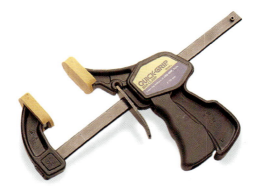

Quick & Easy Furniture *You Can Build With* **Dimensional Lumber**

BLAIR HOWARD

POPULAR WOODWORKING BOOKS
CINCINNATI, OHIO

www.popularwoodworking.com

READ THIS IMPORTANT SAFETY NOTICE

To prevent accidents, keep safety in mind while you work. Use the safety guards installed on power equipment; they are for your protection. When working on power equipment, keep fingers away from saw blades, wear safety goggles to prevent injuries from flying wood chips and sawdust, wear headphones to protect your hearing, and consider installing a dust vacuum to reduce the amount of airborne sawdust in your woodshop. Don't wear loose clothing, such as neckties or shirts with loose sleeves, or jewelry, such as rings, necklaces or bracelets, when working on power equipment. Tie back long hair to prevent it from getting caught in your equipment. People who are sensitive to certain chemicals should check the chemical content of any product before using it. The author and editors who compiled this book have tried to make the contents as accurate and correct as possible. Plans, illustrations, photographs and text have been carefully checked. All instructions, plans and projects should be carefully read, studied and understood before beginning construction. Due to the variability of local conditions, construction materials, skill levels, etc., neither the author nor Popular Woodworking Books assumes any responsibility for any accidents, injuries, damages or other losses incurred resulting from the material presented in this book.

METRIC CONVERSION CHART

TO CONVERT	TO	MULTIPLY BY
Inches	Centimeters	2.54
Centimeters	Inches	0.4
Feet	Centimeters	30.5
Centimeters	Feet	0.03
Yards	Meters	0.9
Meters	Yards	1.1
Sq. Inches	Sq. Centimeters	6.45
Sq. Centimeters	Sq. Inches	0.16
Sq. Feet	Sq. Meters	0.09
Sq. Meters	Sq. Feet	10.8
Sq. Yards	Sq. Meters	0.8
Sq. Meters	Sq. Yards	1.2
Pounds	Kilograms	0.45
Kilograms	Pounds	2.2
Ounces	Grams	28.4
Grams	Ounces	0.04

Quick and Easy Furniture You Can Build With Dimensional Lumber. Copyright © 2000 by Blair Howard. Manufactured in the United States of America. All rights reserved. No part of this book may be reproduced in any form or by any electronic or mechanical means including information storage and retrieval systems without permission in writing from the publisher, except by a reviewer, who may quote brief passages in a review. Published by Popular Woodworking Books, an imprint of F&W Publications, Inc., 1507 Dana Avenue, Cincinnati, Ohio, 45207. First edition.

Visit our Web site at www.popularwoodworking.com for information on more resources for woodworkers.

Other fine Popular Woodworking Books are available from your local bookstore or direct from the publisher.

04   03   02   01   00   5   4   3   2   1

Library of Congress Cataloging-in-Publication Data

Howard, Blair.
    Quick and easy furniture you can build with dimensional lumber / by Blair Howard.
        p. cm.
    Includes index.
    ISBN 1-55870-523-6 (alk. paper)
    1. Furniture making. 2. Woodwork—patterns. I. Title.
TT194.H695 2000   99-042162
684.1'04—dc21   CIP

Edited by Michael Berger
Designed by Brian Roeth
Production coordinated by Emily Gross
Computer illustrations by Blair Howard
Photography by Al Parrish

About the Author

Blair Howard's interest in woodworking began more than forty years ago in high school in England. His interest in furniture, especially antique furniture, goes back even further. Apart from a short stint as a carpenter for a construction company, his woodworking was never more than a sometime hobby. Then, as a result of corporate downsizing, he suddenly found himself looking for work. So, the hobby became a source of income. Today, his work is much in demand and sells to all sorts of markets: galleries, furniture stores, factory outlets and individuals. He lives in Cleveland, Tennessee.

table of contents

Introduction *page 6*

introduction

Over the years I've built a lot of furniture from framing lumber—more than I care to remember. In the early days I used 1x12 pine shelving boards in 16' lengths. From this versatile material I've built tables, chairs, beds, armoires, cupboards, sideboards and a wide range of reproduction antiques. The material is finished on all four sides, relatively flat and free from warp, and—most important—inexpensive. However, it took me a long time to realize that there's more to stock framing lumber than the good old 1x12. I think the light went on one day when I was ripping a board down to 9", complaining under my breath that the offcut, while it wouldn't be wasted, would increase the cost of the finished project by some 15 to 20 percent. I began to wonder if there was a better way.

Of course, I knew that stock lumber came in widths from 12" all the way down to 1". What I didn't realize was that the narrower the board, the less expensive per board foot it became. For instance, I was, at the time, buying shelving board for around 90 cents per board foot. At the lumberyard I found I could buy 1x10 white pine, finished on three sides only, for 63 cents a board foot. Narrower lengths were proportionately cheaper. True, I needed a planer to finish the fourth side, but I already owned a Delta 12" portable planer, so I was able to utilize this new source of inexpensive lumber for no extra investment in tools. The new source of lumber offered an even bigger bonus: The white pine was graded "number 2 common," which meant that it was a better-quality material than the shelving board I'd been used to.

Anyway, the experience started me looking for what else might be available. I made the rounds of lumberyards, builders supply houses, and the great do-it-yourself home center chains. What I found opened up a world of new possibilities and all sorts of wild and wonderful ideas. I was able to create shortcuts and do stuff that previously was beyond the limited scope of my small shop. Slowly, I developed a range of easy-to-build furniture projects—for indoor and outdoor use—that most people would be proud to own.

Just for fun, I decided to take things another step forward. I wondered how much I could do with just a minimum of power and hand tools. I found I could do a lot more than I thought. In fact, I found there was very little I couldn't do with just a table saw, a jigsaw/saber saw, a circular saw, a hammer, a drill, a screwdriver, a couple of chisels and a couple of drill bits. It wasn't too much longer before I realized I had enough ideas, information and projects for a book (perhaps I always had one in the back of my mind)—the book you are now holding in your hands.

This is a book for woodworkers of all skill levels and experience; there's something for just about everyone. For you beginners, you'll find that, with a little thought and application, you will be able to build every project. For you more experienced woodworkers, these projects will provide hours of fun and relaxation. These projects will provide a range of attractive pieces that will enhance any home, yard or garden. Yes, this really is fine furniture you can be proud to show off in your home. All of the pieces can be made using only a few power tools and inexpensive stock lumber. I hope you get as much enjoyment from building these projects as I did.

Choosing Your **Lumber**

Stock framing lumber comes in all sorts of shapes and sizes and from a variety of sources. The one size that probably comes to mind first, the one that even my wife is familiar with, is the 2 x 4. The 2 x 4 is the backbone of the construction industry and thus can be found in various grades, all relatively inexpensive  to buy. But that's just one of many different sizes available. For the projects in this book, we'll be working with softwood. Softwood is cut from evergreen trees, such as pine, spruce, fir, cedar, redwood, and others. Though you can, if you like, build any or all of the projects in this book from hardwood.

Grades of Lumber

Select grade is the best grade of softwood, and it can be expensive. While some select pieces may have some small defects and knots, it is the clearest softwood you can buy. Though it is not generally used as framing lumber, remember that the better the lumber, the better the furniture. Select-grade softwood is not readily available everywhere, certainly not at the major chain stores. You should be able to find it at most lumberyards and specialty lumber outlets.

Common stock (one notch down from select softwood, and the grade I most often use) comes in five subcategories. These subgrades are numbered 1 through 5, with number 1 being the finest, akin to select, and number 5 being the poorest grade, suitable only for construction and framing purposes. Many of the projects in this book are made from number 3 common.

Pressure-Treated Softwood

Pressure-treated lumber is used for most outdoor construction projects where the wood will be exposed to the weather, insects and fungus. Most pressure-treated lumber is impregnated with a waterborne preservative, either chromated copper arsenate or ammoni-

PRESSURE-TREATED LUMBER SAFETY

- Always wear a dust mask.
- Wear gloves, but only when they don't impede your ability to work safely with your power tools.
- Never leave sawdust lying around on the floor.
- Wash dusty clothes separately from other household clothing.
- Keep treated sawdust away from foods, and don't eat or drink in the shop when working with treated wood.
- Never use pressure-treated wood to make toys, cutting boards, turned bowls, kitchen countertops or any other item that might come in contact with food or drink.
- Don't burn pressure-treated wood; the smoke produced can be toxic.

DIMENSIONS

Framing lumber comes in various lengths from 8' long all the way through 16' and, in some cases, even longer. It comes in widths from 2" through 12", and in thickness from 1" through 8", with heavier thicknesses available through special order. Fairly simple so far, right? Well, yes and no. The length you ask for will generally be what you get. As to width and thickness, not so. For example, 2 x 4 is not 2" thick or 4" wide. It was when it started life in the sawmill, but from there it went through several operations, until it became the 2 x 4 we are familiar with. But now, that same 2 x 4 actually measures 1½" x 3½"; it lost some of its bulk between the sawmill and retail outlet. And that's the way it is with all framing lumber and prefinished stock.

acal copper zinc arsenate. When working with treated lumber you should take some basic but necessary precautions (see Pressure-Treated Lumber Safety).

Other Stock Sizes

There are a number of other useful stock items, some of which we'll be using for our projects: dowels, moulding (coves and crowns), rosettes and turnings. Dowels are sold by the piece, usually in 3' and 4' lengths. Moulding is also sold by the piece, but can often be purchased by the linear foot. Turnings (legs, banisters, etc.) and rosettes are also sold by the piece.

Plywood

Like framing lumber, plywood comes in an array of grades, finishes and thicknesses. Most plywood comes in 4' × 8'

TIP *To correctly inspect your prospective lumber, set each board on its narrow side and sight down the edge; it should be straight. Next, turn the board so that its face side is up, hold it at one end and raise the end up to eye level. Squint your eyes and compare the end profile closest to you with the other end. If there's even a hint that it's twisted or warped, discard it.*

Nominal vs. Real Dimensions

STATED DIMENSION	REAL DIMENSION
1 x 2	¾" x 1½"
1 x 3	¾" x 2½"
1 x 4	¾" x 3½"
1 x 6	¾" x 5½"
1 x 8	¾" x 7¼"
1 x 10	¾" x 9¼"
1 x 12	¾" x 11¼"
2 x 2	1½" x 1½"
2 x 4	1½" x 3½"
2 x 6	1½" x 5½"
2 x 8	1½" x 7¼"
2 x 10	1½" x 9¼"
2 x 12	1½" x 11¼"
4 x 4	3½" x 3½"
6 x 6	5½" x 5½"
8 x 8	7¼" x 7¼"

sheets, and in thickness starting at ⅛" and working upward in ⅛" increments. With a few exceptions, we will be concerned only with ¼" lauan plywood and ¾" outdoor-grade plywood. The best place to buy your plywood is at the lumberyard. At the large chains, you'll probably pay twice the lumberyard price or more. An advantage the large chains have over the lumberyards, though, is that they are usually willing to sell you just a half sheet of plywood, whereas the lumberyard, most likely, will not.

Sources

There must be as many good sources for stock framing lumber as there are convenience stores. The most obvious place to buy stock framing lumber is at one of the chain DIY home centers. Though they are probably the most expensive places to buy it, they are convenient, and their range of stock sizes is often impressive.

Your local hardware store can also supply most of your needs, and often at competitive prices compared to the bigger chains. However, your choices and their supply are going to be limited.

Perhaps the best local source is the builder's supply. There you can buy stock framing lumber at prices that may be as much 50 percent lower than the hardware store. You will probably find a good selection of sizes, and you may be able to be more selective in what you purchase.

A final option is the lumberyard or sawmill (this is where I buy most of my stock). I can buy 1×4 treated pine for mere pennies per linear foot, and the rest of the range at comparable prices. A 2×12 costs me about a buck per linear foot.

With all of these options, the best solution is to shop around. Open the yellow pages and look under *lumber*; you'll be surprised at the list. Pick up the phone and make the calls. Visit the sites and see what's available. If you're going to be building a lot of furniture, you might be able to score some better prices, either in quantity or by developing a good buying relationship over time.

BUYING BY BOARD FEET

If you are purchasing a better grade of lumber at a lumberyard or a specialty wood outlet, you most likely will be purchasing by the board foot rather than by the linear foot (as you would at the home improvement store). A board foot equals 144 cubic inches, basically a 1"x12"x12" board. To calculate this measurement, simply multiply the dimensions in inches and divide by 144. For example, your basic 8'-long 2x4 is about 5⅓ board feet (2 x 4 x 96 = 768; 768 divided by 144 = 5.333).

It's most likely that you will be shopping at the local home center-where you will pay by unit price-rather than a lumberyard, so this may not even be a consideration. But if you have the opportunity to purchase better lumber at a lumberyard, you will almost always save money. For example, you might buy a nice (select or #1 common) 10'-long 1x12 pine board at the lumberyard, and it will run close to $2 per board foot and, therefore, will cost about $20. Buy the same size piece of stock at the home center, and you can expect to pay at least the same price, if not more, for a lesser grade of lumber.

TIP *Although framing lumber comes in so-called standard widths and lengths, these do in fact vary somewhat from piece to piece, especially in the smaller widths. These can vary in size by as much as ¼". If you find you are unable to obtain the required width as per one of the cutting lists, it's a simple matter to rip a wide piece to the width you need. Simply use your straightedge and circular saw, or a table saw if you have one.*

What to Look For

The shopping phase is particularly important. How you purchase your lumber will have a direct bearing on how your finished project will look. Always remember to buy the best wood you can afford. While you might be able to get really good prices on stud lumber, if it isn't going to yield the appearance you desire, it's not a bargain.

What this means is that you've got to be selective, even picky. That's probably quite acceptable at the major chain stores where you virtually serve yourself. At the lumberyard, however, you may have to be assertive. Most yardhands will tell you they are not allowed to sort through the stock, and that's often true. But you don't have to buy every piece they show you, and if you feel any particular piece is unacceptable, you should turn it down flat. Explain that you're making furniture, and you'll find most yard staff accommodating.

Framing lumber is usually stored in covered, open-fronted buildings, so it's susceptible to the weather. Untreated lumber will absorb moisture directly out of the air and will lose it on dry days. It will swell, shrink, warp and split. If you can, choose boards from deep within the pile: at least a half-dozen boards down. Store the wood flat in a dry place—your garage or basement—for at least four weeks before you use it. This will give it a chance to dry out somewhat and shrink to something like its final stage. There's nothing worse than to build a nice cabinet, but find a few months down the road that the doors have shrunk a quarter inch, or more.

LUMBER SHOPPING RULES

- Buy the best lumber you can afford.
- Pick and choose your stock. Never accept less than the best of a particular grade of lumber.
- Knots are okay so long as they are small and tight.
- If you can, choose stock from deep within the stack where it will have been somewhat sheltered from the environment.
- Avoid boards that are warped, twisted, bowed or split.
- Plan your shopping trip and buy a little more than you need.

At first sight, any piece of lumber can look deceptively clear (free from knots) and attractive. However, things might not be quite what they seem. Inspect your prospective boards carefully. Splits must be cut away, which means waste. Warps and bows can be straightened, but only with fairly sophisticated machinery, which you may not own, and can take a lot of time to do. While you can cut narrow strips from a split board, the outcome inevitably is waste.

Many of the furniture pieces in this book can be left unfinished—no paint or stain—which means the board itself must be as nice as you can find. Tight knots can be aesthetically pleasing; knotholes never are. Indeed, some country-style projects look better if "knotty pine" is used. For painted projects, however, you can be a little less demanding.

Always plan your shopping trip with care, as it will save you money. If you have to cut away knots and splits, you'll be carving away usable material and will have to go shopping for more to complete the project. To allow for any inevitable mistakes, it's prudent to buy just a little more material than you actually need, perhaps as much as 10 to 30 percent, depending on the project size.

2

Choosing Your **Tools**

When choosing your tools, there is only one real rule: Buy the best you can afford. While all of the projects in this book were built using the simplest tools possible, there's no real need to skimp on tooling, unless cost is the single overriding factor. Few of us have the income where having a fully outfitted professional shop is possible. Most woodworkers start out with simple handheld power tools that find their most frequent uses in home do-it-yourself projects: a drill, a circular saw and a jigsaw or saber saw. And though these tools aren't intended for fine woodworking applications, they will certainly do the job if that is all you can afford.

Drills

Drills can be either a cordless, rechargeable model or a corded version. Whichever you decide upon, it should have variable speeds. I own a Porter-Cable 9.6-volt cordless drill (you can buy more powerful versions, but this one does all I ask it to), a Black & Decker ¼" corded drill, and a Sears Craftsman ⅜" variable-speed corded drill. A variable-speed corded drill can be bought for as little as $35, while a 12-volt cordless model can cost as much as $200. With the numerous models out on the market today, you're bound to find one that falls into your price category.

Table and Circular Saws

You can spend thousands on a professional cabinet saw, but you can also spend a couple hundred on a good benchtop table saw. Remember that you can build this furniture using a circular saw, which is a very versatile and indispensable tool. I own two: a Porter-Cable 7¼" left-hand saw and an older 7¼" Skil saw. You can buy an inexpensive model for as little as $25, or you can pay as much as $175 for one that's considered top of the line.

Jigsaws and Saber Saws

You'll need one of these to cut out those little details that would normally be done on a band saw or scroll saw. There are hundreds of options available to you at prices ranging from as little as $20 all the way up to $200. I own a couple of Porter-Cable models, including one of the new bayonet types. If you decide to buy one of these versatile little saws, be sure to get one that has a tilting base, which comes in handy when cutting bevels.

Hand Tools

When it comes to hand tools, keep it simple. All you'll need is a good quality claw hammer, a basic set of three wood chisels (¼", ½" and 1"), some inexpensive bar clamps (2 each of 12", 24", 36" and 48"), a small backsaw, a miter box, a combination square, a 48" straightedge, and a good quality-tape measure.

The Delta benchtop table saw

Suggested portable power tools

Jigs and Fixtures

A jig makes cutting, milling, drilling or assembling accurate and consistent. Jigs are used mostly when making large numbers of a particular part, or when you need help with repetitive or difficult jobs.

You'll need just one jig for the projects in this book. It's really not much more than a basic T square, but this one is used in combination with your circular saw for long crosscuts or for milling dadoes and rabbets, the primary joint components of many of our projects. It ensures a perfectly square cut and eliminates the need for a radial arm or chop saw (see Making the T-Square Jig).

Glues

For indoor projects, use carpenter's glue, a basic yellow glue that dries fast and hard. Typically, you'll glue, assemble and clamp a piece of furniture, and the glue will cure in less than an hour.

TIP *Always apply glue to both surfaces to be glued, then spread evenly with a small brush. The brush will clean up easily and quickly in water. Having applied the glue, set your clamps, spacing them evenly along the joint (edge-to-edge joint) or at strategic points on the construction. Do not squeeze the joint too tightly. If you do, you'll push most of the glue out of the joint, leaving it starved and weak. Apply just enough pressure to bring the parts tightly together and push a little of the glue out of the joint. Excess pressure will also cause the clamps to damage the surface of the work, especially if you're working with softwoods. Clean away excess glue with a damp rag.*

For outdoor projects, use a weatherproof version of carpenter's glue. It, too, is a yellow glue, but it's mostly impervious to water and weather and takes a little longer to cure. It's advisable to leave the construction in the clamps overnight.

MAKING THE T-SQUARE JIG

Cut the pieces to size, and then lay the small piece on the bench and apply a liberal coating of glue to one side. Place the piece of plywood on top of the smaller piece, positioning it so it is centered and so the bottom edge of the plywood runs perfectly parallel to the bottom edge of the smaller piece. Drive one screw through both pieces. Use your combination square to make sure the two pieces are at exact right angles to each other. Drive another screw through both pieces and again check that the two are square. Then drive the other three screws and allow time for the glue to fully cure. Once the glue has cured, lay the jig across a piece of stock, take your circular saw and make your first crosscut. The saw will take not only the end of the board, but also the end of the exposed portion of the jig, and that's good. The end of your T-square jig will now be perfectly aligned with your circular saw. Do the same with the other side of the jig so that you can use your saw on either side of the jig.

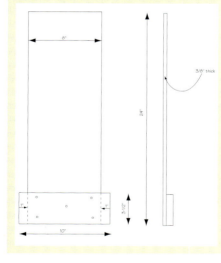

Fasteners

The fasteners we'll use include nails, screws, and a few carriage bolts, washers and nuts. You'll also need a few hinges, knobs, handles and other assorted hardware.

Nails come in all sorts of different shapes and sizes, the most common of which are the "common" nail and the "finishing" nail. The common nail has a large flat head, the finishing nail a small head that can be driven below the surface of the wood leaving a small hole that can easily be filled.

Screws come in almost as wide a variety as nails. The drywall screw is a cheap, easy-to-use screw that will provide a strong joint. Pilot drill and countersink before you insert the screw, and it, too, can be filled and painted over. The deck screw is a galvanized version of the drywall screw and is an adequate fastener for any outdoor project.

Suggested hand tools

You'll need clamps, the more you have the better. This shows what's available.

Cutting List • T-Square Jig

REF.	QTY.	PART	STOCK	THICK	WIDTH	LENGTH	COMMENTS
A	1	Guide	Plywood	$3/8$	8	24	
B	1	Stop	1 x 4	$3/4$	$3\frac{1}{2}$	10	

Hardware							
	5	Wood Screws	#6			1	

3

Construction Techniques

Construction techniques have, for the most part, been reduced to the basics in this book. These projects can be built by anyone, even those with a minimum of tools and experience. Woodworkers with more experience and a wider range of tools, however, can feel free to upgrade the basic techniques to suit themselves. So, with the exception of a few simple joints, most of the projects are assembled and fastened together using glue, screws and, in some instances, nails.

Cutting Techniques

No matter how wide the range of the sizes of framing lumber might be, there will be some sawing to do. You'll need to crosscut (saw the long boards to exact, usable lengths), and in some cases, you'll also need to rip (cut down the length of the board along the grain) your stock to a narrower width. You'll also need to cut shapes: cutouts, decorative curves, etc. All of these involve some specific and exacting techniques. The crosscut must be absolutely square and true, otherwise the structure you build will be twisted and will not stand square. Rips must also run straight and true down the length of the stock. Experienced woodworkers with sophisticated stationary tools—table saw, radial arm saw, chop saw, etc.—have no trouble performing these tasks. But what about us? All we have is a simple, handheld circular saw. The answer is, of course, the T-square jig described in chapter two. If you have made it properly, you can rely on it to constantly produce not only square and true crosscuts, but dadoes, rabbets, and lap joints, as well. Simply put, the technique is to accurately mark the position of the cut, set the depth of cut on your saw, and then make the cut.

Crosscutting

In order to make a straight crosscut, first mark the position of the cut. Set the edge of the jig in line with the mark, then make the cut (see photos 1 and 2).

Ripping

No matter how carefully you choose your stock, there will be the odd occasion when you'll need to rip a board to make it narrower. This is fairly easy to do, provided you take your time. You'll need your circular saw, a couple of clamps and a straightedge (or you can buy a clamp specifically made for this operation—I use a 48" steel rule). Mark the start and finish of the cut. Remove your circular saw from its power source and measure the distance from the inside of the blade to the outer edge of the saw's base. Make marks the same

1 When crosscutting with the T-square jig, line up the outer tip of the jig with the mark where the cut is to be made.

distance inside the start and finish marks you've already made, then place your straightedge on those marks and clamp it at both ends. Set the edge of the saw's base against the straightedge and then carefully make the cut (see photos 3 and 4).

Dadoes and Rabbets

The dado is a relatively simple joint to make, even with our limited range of tools. It's also one of the strongest of the joints we'll make. This type of joint is used mostly for securing shelving to the outer walls of cupboards, cabinets and the like. The dado is simply a slot milled into one board into which the end of the board to be joined is tightly fitted. The secret to a good dado joint is to make sure the dado itself is not cut too wide, thus making for a sloppy fit. To reinforce dadoes, you can use dowels, biscuits, screws or nails. You can see exactly how this joint can be made using your circular saw, T-square jig and chisel in the step-by-step photos in this chapter.

A rabbet is essentially a dado, but made either along the edge of a board or at the end. It's made in exactly the same way as the dadoes, using the same tools, jig and techniques. It does, however, allow a little more leeway for error because the joining board is laid into the rabbet rather than fitting tightly into a slot. I always reinforce the joint, either with screws or finishing nails.

To make either a dado or rabbet, first mark both outer limits of the intended cut. Set the edge of the T-square jig on the stock in line with the

2 Either hold the jig firmly in place or secure it with a clamp and then make the cut.

3 You can rip down the grain using your jigsaw and straightedge. Just find the distance from the edge of the saw's base to the blade, make the appropriate marks on the work, clamp the straightedge in position, and make the cut.

4 By far the quickest way to rip down the grain is to use your circular saw. This technique is best used on wide boards, but is basically the same as you would use if you were using a jigsaw. The distance between the edge of the saw's base and the blade will be different, however, and you will need to take that into consideration.

5 The same technique applies here as with crosscutting, but this time you'll set the depth of cut to that required for the dado and then make several cuts across the piece instead of just one. When the cuts are complete, clean out any waste that might remain with a chisel.

SQUARING A BOX OR CABINET

Many of the projects in this book require that you build a box-shaped structure. It might be a chest or a bookcase, or it might be the understructure for a cabinet. It's essential that these units are made perfectly square. If they are not square, the unit may stand properly, but the doors, drawers or top will not because the underlying frame will be twisted. You might think you can be sure a piece is square by trying one of the corners with a combination or set square; not so. Often a square will not be exactly true, and any aberration will be greatly exaggerated over a long length. The only reliable way to make sure such a structure is square and true is to set the structure on its back and measure diagonally first from one corner to

the other, make note of the number, then measure the other diagonal. If the unit is square the numbers will be exactly the same. If they are not, you'll need to square, the structure by applying pressure, with a clamp, diagonally across the longer dimension, measuring as you go.

inside of the furthest of the two marks—you'll work your way back toward the other mark. Keep in mind that your jig is set up to make your saw cut on the waste side of the marks; you may have to adjust your mark or the jig to cut the outer limits correctly. Set the depth of the circular saw blade to cut at the required depth, say ⅜". Make the first cut across the stock. Move the jig ⅛" toward the second limiting mark on the stock and make a second cut. Repeat the process until you have cleared out the entire dado, and then clean the resulting recess carefully with a chisel (see photo 5).

Lap Joint

The lap joint is a simple joint, quite similar to the dado joint, but it's used almost exclusively to join cross members together; that is, two or more narrow strips of stock in the form of a cross. The main difference is that instead of one slot into which the joining board must fit, the lap requires two slots, each exactly equal in width to the two pieces to be joined, into which both pieces fit, one over the other.

The technique for making a lap joint with the T-square jig and a circular saw is essentially the same as that for making a dado; you simply do it twice. First mark the position of the lap on both

pieces of stock. Set the depth of cut on your circular saw to exactly half the thickness of one of the two pieces of stock. Be extra careful performing this step; if you go too deep, you'll end up with a step in the joint that will be almost impossible to eliminate. Practice on some scrap pieces of stock to get the depth of cut exactly right. Having set the depth of cut correctly, set the jig on the first piece of stock to cut inside the line farthest away—you'll work your way back toward the other mark. Now make your first cut. Move the jig ⅛" toward the second mark and make another cut. Continue the process, making cut after cut until you've cleared away the entire lap. Then, repeat the process on the second piece of stock.

Butt Joint

This is the simplest of all woodworking joints; it's also the weakest, unless you reinforce it with screws, nails, dowels or biscuits. Two pieces of wood are simply glued together at right angles, then clamped until the glue has fully cured.

Edge-to-Edge Joint

This is the method we'll use to make large, flat boards from two or more narrow boards. The edges are glued, and

then the boards are clamped together tightly until the glue has fully cured.

There's a lot of controversy about whether or not it's necessary to reinforce this type of joint with dowels, biscuits or splines (long strips of wood set in grooves between two boards, rather like a tongue-and-groove system). Now, while I believe you should reinforce this type of joint if you can, I've never had a plain, unreinforced edge-to-edge joint break down. I find it to be absolutely true that the wood on either side of a properly glued edge-to-edge joint will break before the glue does.

Miter Joint

The miter joint, unless reinforced, is one of the weakest joints. It, too, is a fairly simple joint to make, but the 45° angles (or miters) must be cut accurately in order for it to work. Having cut the miters accurately, it's simply a matter of applying glue and carefully clamping the assembly until the glue has fully cured.

4

Small
Cupboard

This neat little cupboard is ideal for the kitchen, a child's bedroom, or even a living room. It's made from a combination of 1 x 10, 1 x 8 and 1 x 2 stock framing lumber. Other than for the plywood back and the door, there's no ripping involved; you can use the wood just as it comes. The only joints involved here are the dado and rabbet joints that hold the shelves and top into the two side sections, and a simple edge-to-edge joint for the two pieces that make up the door. The trim is applied to the case using finishing nails and glue.

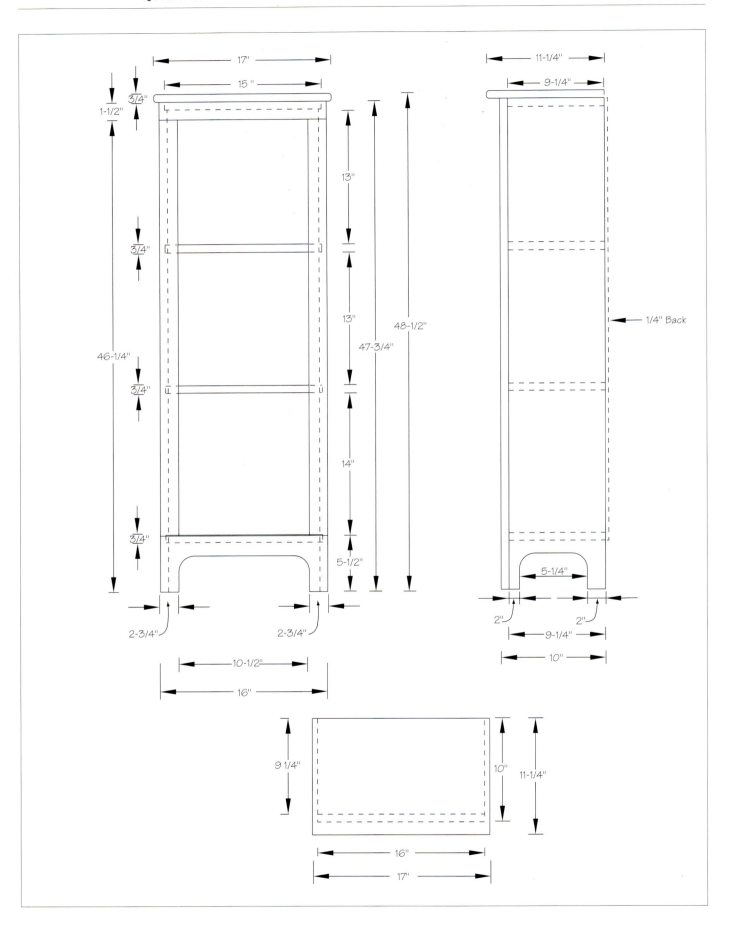

Cutting List • Small Cupboard

REF.	QTY.	PART	STOCK	THICK	WIDTH	LENGTH	COMMENTS
	2	Sides	1 x 10	$3/4$	$9 1/4$	$47 3/4$	
	4	Shelves	1 x 10	$3/4$	$9 1/4$	15	
	1	Top	1 x 12	$3/4$	$11 1/4$	17	
	1	Door	1 x 8	$3/4$	13	$39 1/4$	Edge-join two pieces
	2	Trim	1 x 2	$3/4$	$1 1/2$	$39 1/4$	
	1	Trim	1 x 2	$3/4$	$1 1/2$	16	
	1	Trim	1 x 6	$3/4$	$5 1/2$	16	
	3	Door Cleats	1 x 2	$3/4$	$1 1/2$	11	
	1	Back	Plywood	$1/4$	16	$40 3/4$	

Hardware

	1 pr.	Decorative Hinges					
	1	Decorative Knob					
	1	Door Catch					
		Finishing Nails	6D				
		Drywall Screws				$1 1/4$	
		Brads				1	

Supplies

		Carpenter's Glue					

REQUIRED TOOLS

Table or circular saw

Jig saw, saber saw or band saw

T-Square jig

Combination square

Hammer

Nail set

Sander (or sandpaper and block)

Steel straightedge

Screwdriver

Chisel

Clamps

Measuring Tape

Drill

Construction

After cutting all the pieces to length as indicated in the cutting chart, carefully lay out the positions of the dadoes and rabbets on the two side panels that will receive the shelves and the top (see photo 1). Mill the dadoes and rabbets in the side panels, and clean the cuts with a chisel (see photos 2 and 3).

1 Lay out the positions of the dadoes and rabbets on the two side panels that will receive the shelves and the top.

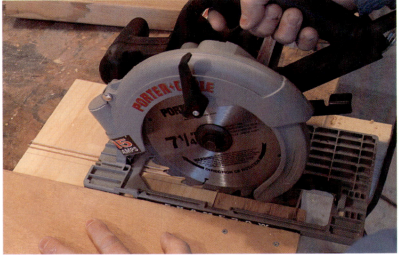

2 With your circular saw, mill the dadoes and rabbets in the side panels.

3 Clean the cuts out with a chisel.

4 **Use any round bottle to help you draw the cutouts for the feet.**

5 **Use your jigsaw to make the cutouts first for the feet . . .**

6 **. . . and then for the decorative front trim.**

Lay out the decorative cutouts that will form the feet. If you don't have a compass handy to draw the curves, trace around any round bottle that has a pleasing curve (see photo 4). Then use your jigsaw to make the cutouts for the feet and for the front trim (see photos 5 and 6).

7 Run a bead of glue in the rabbet and dadoes where you'll mount the false top and shelves.

8 Mount the false top and shelves into the rabbet and dadoes. Use screws to reinforce the mounting.

9 Lay the cupboard on its back and measure the diagonals to ensure that the structure is square.

Glue and assemble the shelves and false top to the sides (see photos 7 and 8). Then lay the structure on its back and measure the diagonals to ensure that the structure is square (see photo 9). Then use 1" brads to fasten the plywood back to the case.

Using glue and finishing nails, attach the trim to the case. Apply the top rail first, then the two stiles, and finally the bottom piece (see photo 10). Make sure that you fill any nail holes, so that your surface is smooth and free from marks.

Glue and clamp together your door pieces to make one panel for the door; set the panel aside until the glue has fully cured. If you intend to paint the finished piece, you can use any combination of sizes to make your door the correct width: 1×12 plus 1×4, or 1×10 plus 1×6, and so on.

Measure the door opening in the case, and then trim the door to fit the opening. Do this by using a straight-edge along the full length of the door to guide your circular saw. If the height needs to be trimmed, you can do it by using your T-square jig and circular saw.

To add strength and reduce the effects of wood movement, attach cleats to the inside of the door using drywall screws (see photo 11). Then fasten the knob to the door. Then attach the false top with drywall screws from the inside. Make sure it sits square and cen-

tered on the case (see photo 12).

When all the glue has fully cured, sand all the outer surfaces smooth using 80-grit sandpaper first, then 150-grit to finish. Apply a coat of primer to all the outer surfaces, and allow it to dry thoroughly, preferably overnight. Then apply one or two coats of gloss or semigloss paint as necessary. If you like, apply decoration to the door using a stencil purchased from a craft or hardware store. Finally, attach the hinges to the door, set the door in place in its opening, fasten the hinges to the trim and mount the catch in place.

10 Use finishing nails to attach your trim pieces.

11 Attach cleats to the inside of the door to add strength and protect against wood movement.

TIP *You can minimize the chances of splitting narrow pieces of wood when you drive in a nail by first dulling the point of the nail with your hammer.*

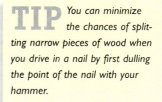

12 Attach the false top with drywall screws from the inside.

5

Blanket
Chest

For thousands of years, chests have been a staple of home furnishing. In medieval times the chest was used for seating, storage and even as a table. Later, it became the symbol of young womanhood: the dower chest. It's still an important furnishing in most homes today. Construction for this chest is quite simple, but requires time and thought. The sides, lid, ends and bottom are made from two pieces of stock lumber edge-glued together. The feet can either be mitered together at the corners or simply butt-jointed. Because wide panels are used in this project, consider using cleats to join the sides to the ends.

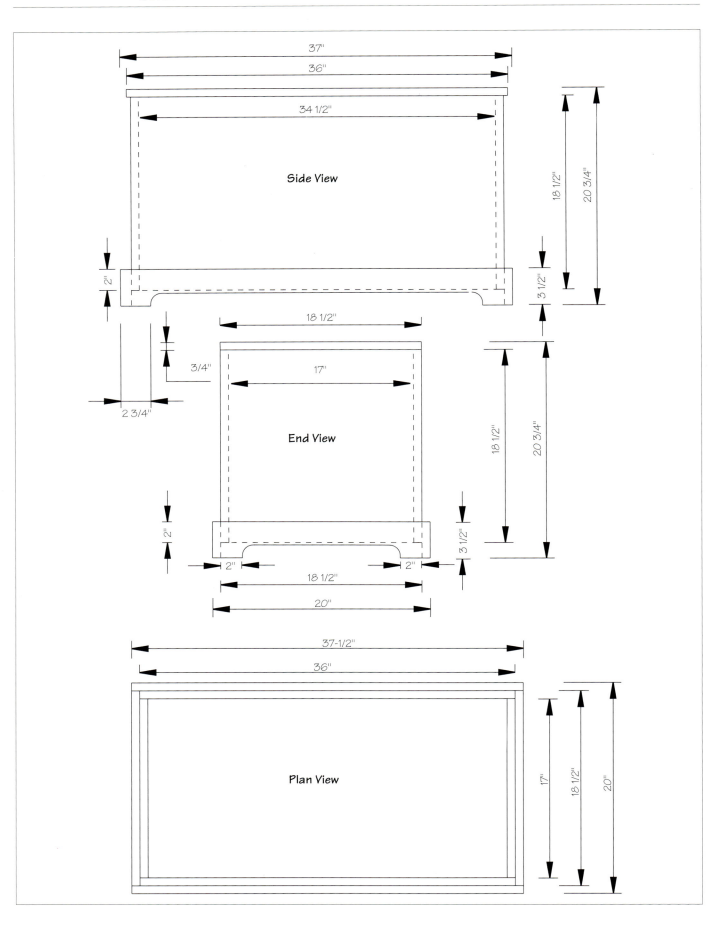

Cutting List • Blanket Chest

REF.	QTY.	PART	STOCK	THICK	WIDTH	LENGTH	COMMENTS
	2	Sides	1x10	$3/4$	$18^1/_2$	36	
	2	Ends	1x10	$3/4$	17	$18^1/_2$	
	1	Bottom	1x10	$3/4$	17	$34^1/_2$	
	1	Top	1x12	$3/4$	$18^1/_2$	37	
	2	Battens	1x2	$3/4$	$1^1/_2$	16	
	8	Cleats	Scrap	$3/4$	$3/4$	4	Use offcuts or rip a 1x2 in half
	2	Side Feet	1x4	$3/4$	$3^1/_2$	$37^1/_2$	
	2	End Feet	1x4	$3/4$	$3^1/_2$	$18^1/_2$	

Hardware

REF.	QTY.	PART	STOCK	THICK	WIDTH	LENGTH	COMMENTS
	1 pr	Steel Hinges					
		Finishing Nails	6D				
		Drywall Screws				$1^1/_4$	

Supplies

REF.	QTY.	PART	STOCK	THICK	WIDTH	LENGTH	COMMENTS
		Carpenter's Glue					
		Wood Putty					

REQUIRED TOOLS

Table or circular saw

Jigsaw, saber saw or band saw

T-square jig

Combination square

Drill

Hammer

Nail set

Screwdriver

Sander (or sandpaper and block)

Steel straightedge

Clamps

Measuring tape

USING CLEATS TO COUNTER WOOD MOVEMENT

Regardless of how picky you are in selecting your stock and in letting it dry thoroughly, wood will move as humidity changes. Granted, your wood selection, joinery and finishing will help reduce this effect, but you simply cannot stop it. The fact that these projects are made from pine and that this particular project uses such wide panels only increases the odds of wood movement.

Whenever you expect dramatic wood movement, you can counter it simply by using cleats. A cleat is a small piece of wood with elongated screw holes drilled in it that will allow the pieces that it is joining to move. You will still attach the pieces with screws, and the joint will remain tight, but when the wood begins to swell or contract with changes in humidity, the screws will allow limited movement within the elongated holes.

In order to determine where cleats are needed, check the grain direction of the pieces to be joined. If the grain runs parallel from one piece to another, you won't need a cleat. If the grain direction is perpendicular, you'll need one.

1 The sides, ends, bottom and lid are made using more than one piece of wood. Create these pieces by making an edge-to-edge joint. Simply apply glue to both edges, then clamp them together until the glue has fully cured.

2 Mark out the radii of the feet sections using either a compass or, as I did, a small can. The dimension is not important; just make sure it looks good to you.

3 Clamp the two sections together and then cut them both using your jigsaw. By cutting both pieces together, you ensure that they are identical.

Construction Steps

After cutting all the pieces to size as indicated in the materials list, build up the boards for the sides, ends, bottom and top by using simple edge-to-edge joints. Make sure you apply the glue evenly to both edges, and don't clamp them too tightly—they should be tight enough only to squeeze a small amount of glue from the joint. If you do it right, the joint will be stronger than the wood itself (see photo 1).

Once your glued-up boards are dry, lay one of the side pieces on your bench and mark the position for the cleats. Stand one of the end pieces on the side piece and make the corresponding marks for the cleat. Attach the

cleats to the side piece using screws and then attach the end piece to the cleat. Repeat the process for the other end. Then stand the unit on its bottom on the floor and attach the second side with cleats.

Set the resulting box on its top on the bench and measure the diagonals to ensure the box is perfectly square. If not, you must make adjustments now, by adding a clamp across the opening and squeezing the long dimension. If the box is not square, the top and bottom won't fit properly in place. Once you're sure everything is square, attach the bottom board to the sides and ends using screws. Use elongated screw holes to accommodate the wood move-

ment of such a large solid panel.

Take the four pieces of 1×2 stock that will form the feet and mark the cutouts. The size of the radius for each cutout is not critical. If you don't have a compass you can use a small jar as I have (see photo 2). Use your jigsaw to make the cutouts, and then sand the pieces smooth; it will be easier to sand the profiles now rather than after attaching them to the chest (see photo 3).

Use glue and finishing nails to fasten the feet in position (see photos 4 and 5). The top of the cutouts should run parallel to the underside of the chest. Make sure you glue the butt joints.

4 Attach the foot pieces. Use glue on the ends and fasten them in place with finishing nails.

5 Use your hammer and a nail set to sink the nail heads below the surface of the wood. Fill the holes with putty and, when it's dry, sand the surface smooth.

6 Predrill pilot holes in the cleats that you'll use to reinforce the inside of the lid.

Set the top board, underside up, on the bench and fasten the two battens in place using drywall screws (see photos 6 and 7). Then set the top in place on the chest and secure it using two steel hinges along the back edge (see photo 8). Finally, sand as necessary to prepare the piece for finishing (see photo 9). To finish the piece, you can either stain or paint it. I chose to paint this one and add a decorative stencil.

7 Use 1¼" drywall screws to fasten the cleats to the inside of the lid; do not use glue.

8 Fasten the hinges to the back edge of the lid and box using the screws provided with the hinges.

9 Finish the piece by sanding all the surfaces smooth. Start with 80-grit sandpaper and finish with 150-grit.

6

Box **Planter**

This planter is the ideal shape and size for a small deck or patio and will provide a much more attractive alternative to the cheap plastic pots I see everywhere. This is one of the easiest projects to construct. Everything is held together with waterproof carpenter's glue and galvanized finishing nails. Each leg is made from two pieces of stock, one 3½" wide and one 1½" wide. The narrow piece is glued, then fastened to the other piece with a butt joint and nails. Everything else follows along in a natural sequence of events as laid out below. You should be able to make one of these in just a couple of hours.

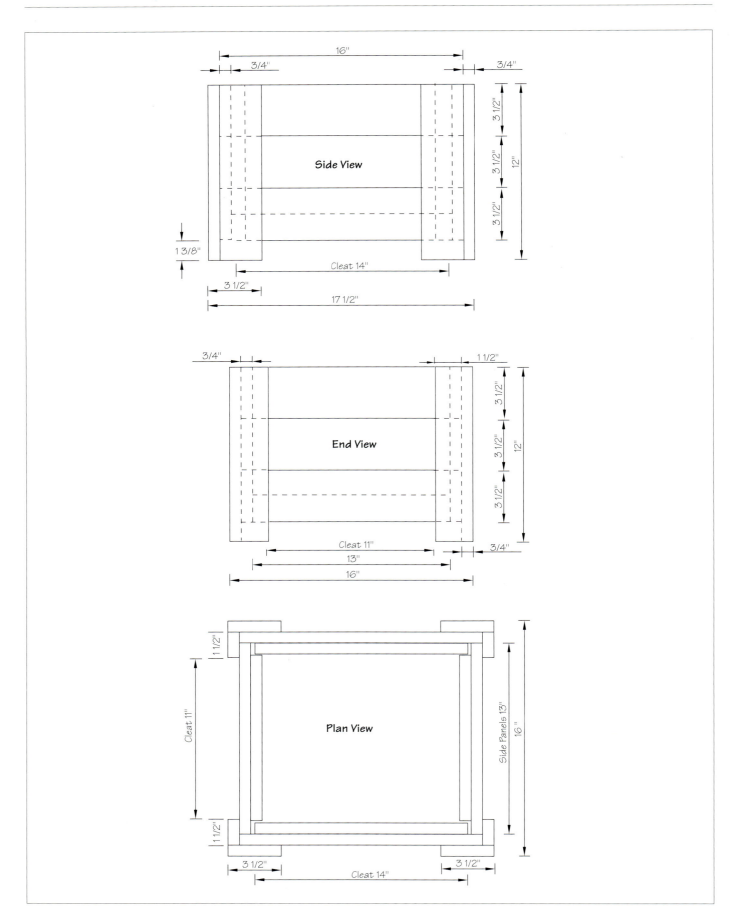

Side View

End View

Plan View

Cutting List • Box Planter

REF.	QTY.	PART	STOCK	THICK	WIDTH	LENGTH	COMMENTS
	4	Legs	1x4	$\frac{3}{4}$	$3\frac{1}{2}$	12	
	4	Legs	1x2	$\frac{3}{4}$	$1\frac{1}{2}$	12	
	6	Long Sides	1x4	$\frac{3}{4}$	$3\frac{1}{2}$	16	
	6	Short Sides	1x4	$\frac{3}{4}$	$3\frac{1}{2}$	13	
	2	Long Cleats	1x2	$\frac{3}{4}$	$1\frac{1}{2}$	14	
	2	Short Cleats	1x2	$\frac{3}{4}$	$1\frac{1}{2}$	11	
	1	Bottom	Plywood	$\frac{3}{4}$	13	15	Use a marine- or exterior-grade plywood

Hardware

		Waterproof liner or sealant					
		Galvanized Finishing Nails	No. 6				

Supplies

		Waterproof Carpenter's Glue					

REQUIRED TOOLS

Table or circular saw

Jigsaw, saber saw or band saw

T-square jig

Combination square

Drill

Hammer

Nail set

Sander (or sandpaper and block)

Steel straightedge

Clamps

Measuring tape

1 The legs for this piece are made from two pieces of stock glued and nailed together. Apply glue to the edge of one piece, then drive in some number 6 finishing nails.

Construction Steps

Cut all the pieces to size as per the materials list and, with 80-grit sandpaper, round over the edges of the 12 side pieces to give them definition once the piece is assembled and painted.

Glue, nail and clamp the leg pieces together (see photo 1). Next, take two legs and three of the long sides and lay them out (see photo 2) to form the first of the two long sides. Glue and nail the side stretchers in place inside the legs. Repeat these steps to form the other long side (see photo 3).

Glue and nail the two long cleats along the inside bottom edges of the two long sides; these will form the supports for the plywood bottom (see photo 4). Set the two sides on edge facing each other, then glue and nail three of the short side pieces in place to form one of the two ends. Repeat these steps to form the second end.

2 Apply glue to one inside face and begin placing the side pieces. These can be fastened in place with nails.

3 Complete the two sides and then fasten the cleats that will support the bottom in place using glue and nails.

Fasten the two short cleats in place along the inside bottom edges of the two ends to complete the support for the bottom. Set the completed box section on its feet on the bench and measure the diagonals to ensure that it is square (see photo 5). Take the piece of plywood that will form the bottom and glue it in place inside the planter on its supports.

Sand everything smooth; remove the sharp corners from the top edges and the edges of all four legs, then apply at least two coats of exterior-quality primer. Apply a couple of coats of exterior-finish paint in a color of your choice, and all that remains is to fill it with earth and choose the plants.

TIP *Before you can fill the planter with earth you'll need to line it somehow. There are all sorts of proprietary brands of waterproofer on the market, and a couple of coats of one of those will work quite well. However, if you combine the waterproofing with a plastic liner, your planter will be sure to give many years of service.*

4 Set the two sides on edge and fasten the side pieces in place between them.

5 Before you fasten the bottom panel in place, make sure the box is square.

7

Country
Bookcase

This bookcase is pure country and quite simple to construct. There's no ripping involved, and you should be able to build it with just a couple of power tools, a hammer and a handful of hardware. The shelves and top are dadoed and rabbeted to the sides. The trim is glued to the carcass and can be reinforced with finishing nails if you wish. Leave the nail heads showing for a country look, or fill the holes with a stainable putty. The doors are simple boards with cleats on the backsides to minimize warping, and the crown is no more than three pieces of stock with the front edges rounded over.

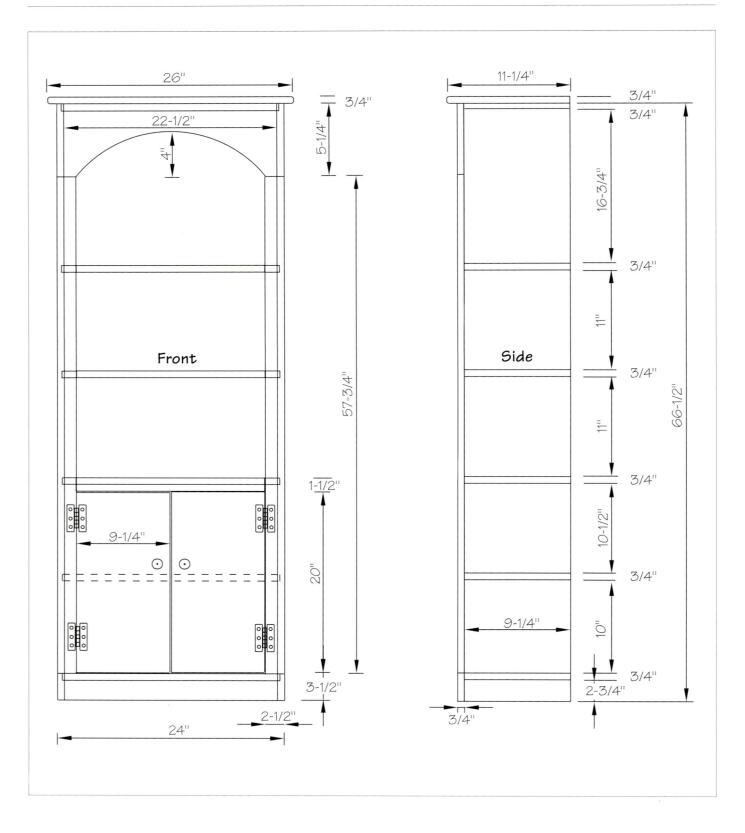

Cutting List • Country Bookcase

REF.	QTY.	PART	STOCK	THICK	WIDTH	LENGTH	COMMENTS
	2	Sides	1x10	3/4	9 1/4	66 1/2	
	6	Shelves and Top	1x12	3/4	9 1/4	23	
	1	Top Trim	1x6	3/4	5 1/4	24	
	1	Bottom Trim	1x4	3/4	3 1/2	24	
	1	Middle Trim	1x2	3/4	1 1/2	19	
	2	Side Trim	1x3	3/4	2 1/2	57 3/4	
	2	Doors	1x10	3/4	9 1/4	20	
	4	Cleats	1x2	3/4	1 1/2	8	
	1	Back	Plywood	3/4	24	66 1/2	

Hardware

	2 prs.	Hinges					
	2	Knobs					
		Finishing Nails	6D				
		Drywall Screws				1 1/2	

Supplies

		Carpenter's Glue					

REQUIRED TOOLS

Table or circular saw

Jigsaw, saber saw or band saw

T-square jig

Combination square

Drill

Hammer

Nail set

Screwdriver

Sander (or sandpaper and block)

Steel straightedge

Chisel

Clamps

Measuring tape

Construction Steps

Cut all the boards to size as indicated in the materials list (see photo 1). Lay out the positions of the dadoes in the side sections. It's best to lay both pieces side by side on the bench and then mark them as one piece. This way you can be sure the two sides match exactly (see photo 2). Mill the dadoes and rabbets in the two sides. These should be about ¼" deep.

Sand all of the pieces smooth, including the doors. If you like, you can even stain everything prior to assembly. This is easier do at this stage than it is when the piece is fully assembled (see photo 3).

Glue, assemble and clamp the shelves and top to the sides. To strengthen the joint, you may want to use biscuits, dowels, screws or nails. Then measure the diagonals to ensure the carcass is square (see photo 4). Make any necessary adjustments, then set it aside until the glue has cured, preferably overnight. Once the glue has fully cured, remove the clamps from the carcass and lay it on its back.

1 Mark out the length of each piece in the cutting list and set your T-square to the mark. It will help if you secure the far edge with a clamp. Then carefully cut all the pieces to length using your circular saw.

2 To ensure accuracy, mark the positions of both sets of dadoes at the same time.

3 If you are going to stain the piece when it's finished, it's best that you don't use nails to fasten the trim to the case. Use glue and clamps instead, but be sure to give the glue time to fully cure.

4 When the case is fully constructed it should look like this. As you can see, the more clamps you have, the better.

Mark out the detail on the top section of trim. Using your jigsaw, cut the detail into the top piece of trim. Use glue and clamps to fasten the trim to the front of the carcass and set it aside until the glue has fully cured; you can reinforce it with finishing nails if you like. If you're using nails, you can either leave the nail heads showing for a country look, or you can set the heads and fill the holes with a stainable putty (see photo 5).

Lay the doors back side up on the bench and lay out the position of the braces or cleats. Use four screws only—no glue—to fasten each brace in position (see photos 6 and 7).

Turn the doors faceup and lay out the position of the knobs and drill the holes. Attach the doorknobs and then sand the edges of the doors smooth before fastening them to the case. Apply the stain and a coat of satin polyurethane. Lastly, attach the hinges to the doors, and then attach the doors to the carcass.

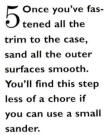

5 Once you've fastened all the trim to the case, sand all the outer surfaces smooth. You'll find this step less of a chore if you can use a small sander.

6 Pre-drill the cleats that will reinforce the cupboard doors.

7 Use 1½" drywall screws to fasten the cleats to the inside of the doors. Do not use glue.

SANDING AND FINISHING

The final look of your piece will only be as good as the preparation you do before you apply the finish. Proper sanding is the secret to a good finish. Now, let me say this: I hate sanding, but it's the one process you can't skip, or even skimp on, if you want your finished project to look good.

You can certainly do your sanding by hand using a sanding block and an assortment of papers—if you enjoy pain, that is. Better, you can buy a finishing sander and make the job a little easier. Start your sanding with a coarse paper, say 80-grit, and work your way through grades 120 and 150. For a really fine finish, use a 220-grit paper.

Sealing Knots

Pine often has a lot of knots. If you plan to leave the knots showing, you need to do little more than sand, stain and apply a clear protective coat of varnish or polyurethane. However, if you intend to paint the project, you'll need to do something more. Knots tend to bleed through a finish; that is, in addition to being darker than the surrounding wood, they will soak up the finish and show through. The bleeding will show through most of the lighter colors, especially white and light blue. So, you need to seal the knots with a few coats of shellac. Simply apply one coat, let it dry thoroughly, and then apply another. Then lightly sand the outer surfaces, apply a coat of primer and then the final color.

Stain

Staining isn't rocket science. Go to the local hardware store, check out the proprietary brands, choose a color you like, and that's about it. To apply stain, simply use a brush—one about 3" wide will do nicely—and spread it using long, even strokes along the grain. Leave it on for about five minutes, then wipe it dry with a soft cloth—an old towel is ideal. Leave it overnight to dry completely, then apply a coat of clear polyurethane for protection.

Paint

There's really nothing difficult about painting by hand. All you need to remember is that paint should always be applied over at least one coat of primer. Almost always you'll need to apply at least two coats of color, allowing plenty of time between coats; each coat should be fully cured before the next is applied, and should be lightly sanded, preferably with 220-grit paper or finer.

For most paint jobs, a quality latex paint will produce great results. However, there are some jobs that may require something spectacular. For those jobs, I recommend you use an oil-based product. It's easy to apply and dries to the touch in about two hours. True, you'll need to purchase some paint thinner for cleanup, but the end result is well worth the little extra effort you have to put into it. Don't be tempted to use water-based polyurethanes. Though they are environmentally friendly, dry fairly quickly and are easy to clean up, they don't provide the results you'll be looking for.

Brushes

I buy foam brushes by the case and use them for all sorts of finishing jobs: stain, latex paint and polyurethane. In bulk, they are cheap enough that I can use them once, then throw them away. However, you should buy a good-quality nylon brush for fine latex painting—the nylon bristles won't absorb water and swell—and a good-quality bristle brush for your oil-based paint.

TIP *If you decide to use a water-based stain, keep in mind that it will raise the grain, which then must be sanded smooth. Most of the proprietary brands of stain are oil based and don't raise the grain at all.*

8

Storage
Step Stool

This is a neat little project you can make over a weekend. It can serve as a purely decorative piece, or you can use it to store things such as shoe polish or brushes. Though a bit complicated, this project is well within the capabilities of anyone with just some basic woodworking

skills, provided you take the time to think it through as you go. The complicated parts are the angles. Just remember 5 degrees, and you won't go wrong. The sides of the legs are angled 5°; the tops and bottoms of the legs are beveled at 5°; and the tops and bottoms of the sides are beveled at 5°.

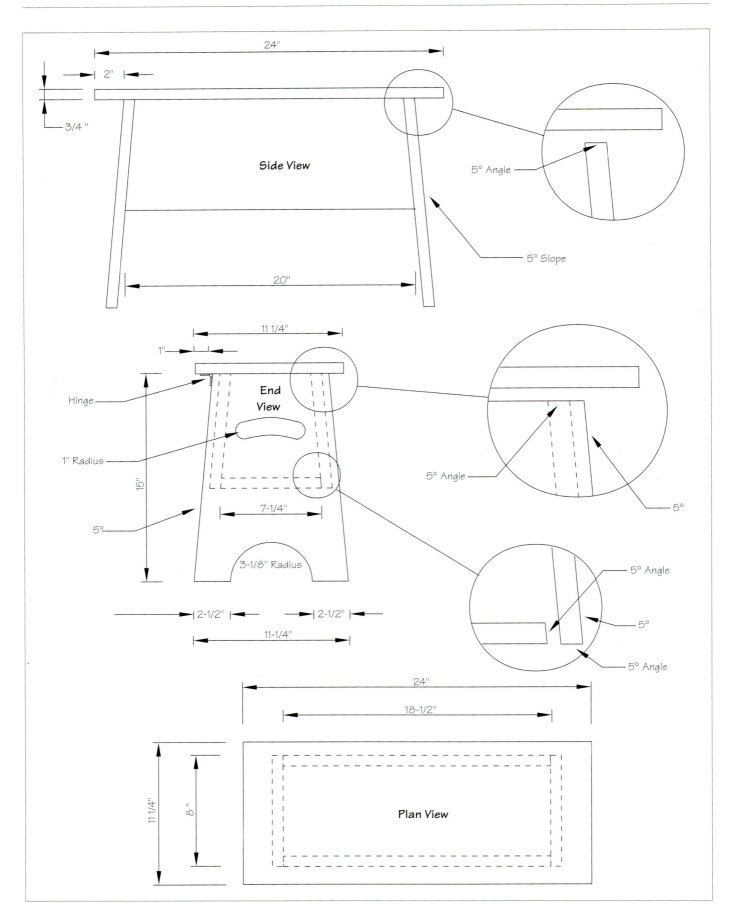

Cutting List • Storage Step Stool

REF.	QTY.	PART	STOCK	THICK	WIDTH	LENGTH	COMMENTS
	2	Legs	1x12	$3/4$	$11^{1}/4$	15	
	2	Sides	1x8	$3/4$	$7^{1}/4$	20	
	1	Bottom	1x8	$3/4$	$7^{1}/4$	20	
	1	Top	1x12	$3/4$	$11^{1}/4$	24	

Hardware

	1 pr.	Butt Hinges	Brass			1	
		Drywall Screws				$1^{1}/4$	
		Wood Screws					
		Finishing Nails	No. 6				

Suplies

		Carpenter's Glue					
		Wood Putty					

REQUIRED TOOLS

Table or circular saw

Jigsaw, saber saw or band saw

Hacksaw

Combination square

Drill

Hammer

Nail set

Screwdriver

Sander (or sandpaper and block)

Steel straightedge

Clamps

Measuring tape

Construction Steps

Cut the pieces to length, except for the legs. Then set the base of your circular saw to an angle of 5° and cut the two leg sections to length. Lay out the feet cutouts, side slopes, and the center points of the two 1"-diameter holes that will form the outer limits of the handles on the outside of just one of the leg pieces. Remember that the legs will lean inward, so the top of the legs will have the point of the beveled edges on the inside.

Use two wood screws to fasten the two end sections together back-to-back so that the top beveled edges meet in a point (see photo 1). Do this somewhere inside what will become the handles, but be sure to allow clearance for drilling the 1"-diameter holes.

Clamp a straightedge in place and, with your jigsaw, cut the first of the two edges down the length (see photo 2). Repeat the process for the other angle. Then, cut out the foot detail (see photo 3).

Use a 1" spade bit to form the outer limits of the handles (see photos 4 and 5). Then with your jigsaw, finish cutting out the handles. This will cause the two sides to separate (see photos 6 and 7). Sand the handle holes smooth, and ease any sharp corners.

Set your circular saw to an angle of 5°. Set your straightedge so that you can trim the top and bottom edges of the two sides just as you did for the ends of the leg sections. Repeat the process for the bottom section. This time, however, you will need to reverse the board for the second cut; the two angles should oppose each other (see the end detail in the drawing).

Use glue and clamps to fasten the two sides to the bottom. When dry, turn the structure upside down. Apply glue to the ends, clamp the two leg sections into position and allow time for the glue to cure. Reinforce the joints between the legs and the box with finishing nails. Set the heads, fill the holes and sand everything smooth.

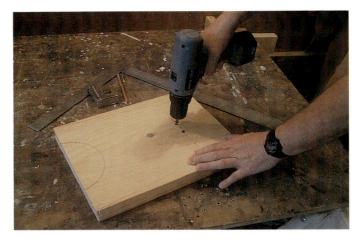

1 Use two screws to fasten the two end sections together. Do this somewhere inside what will become the handles, but be sure to allow clearance for drilling the 1"-diameter holes.

2 Use your straightedge and jigsaw to cut the slopes to the two edges.

3 Now use your jigsaw to cut out the feet.

4 Drill the two 1"-diameter holes through both boards, but drill only deep enough for the point of the spade bit to just break through on the other side of the second board.

5 Reverse the board and complete the drilling of the 1"-diameter holes from the reverse side. This will ensure a clean hole with no ragged edges.

6 Now you can mark out the rest of the handle shape. You can use a compass if you like, but it's easy enough to do freehand. Do not cut the waste out yet.

7 Complete the cutouts for the handles. When the waste drops away, the two end sections will separate, leaving you with two identical pieces. Then it's simply a matter of nailing all the pieces together and filling the nail holes.

Sand the top smooth and ease its sharp edges. Set the top on the bench, underside up, and then set the box section in place on top of it.

Take your 1" brass butt hinge and, using a hacksaw, cut it in half; this will result in two small hinges that will fit on the edges of the two leg sections. Fasten the top to the understructure using the two halves of the brass butt hinge. Fasten them to the edges of the leg sections. If you fasten them to the box sides, the top won't open, because the sides are inset and the tops of the legs will be a solid restriction.

9

Window
Box

There's something about a window box. It dresses up a window and provides endless hours of gardening. This is a small one, as these things go, but you can adjust the dimensions to suit your needs. If you do decide to make it larger, all you need do is change the length. As it is, it can be used indoors or out, provided you line the interior with a plastic, waterproof liner and you keep the plants in their pots. It's ideal for bedding plants, cacti or small ferns. Construction couldn't be simpler; everything is fastened together with waterproof glue and galvanized deck screws. The shaped support brackets are made with a jigsaw.

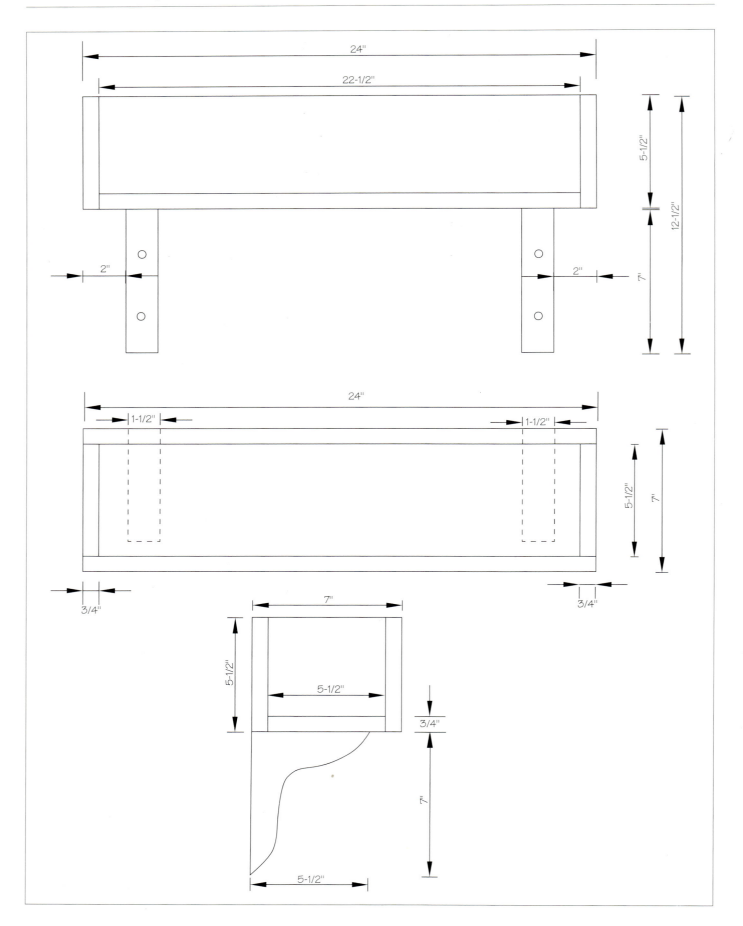

Cutting List • Window Box

REF.	QTY.	PART	STOCK	THICK	WIDTH	LENGTH	COMMENTS
	2	Sides	1x6	$3/4$	$5^1/2$	24	Use pressure-treated lumber
	2	Ends	1x6	$3/4$	$5^1/2$	$5^1/2$	
	1	Bottom	1x6	$3/4$	$5^1/2$	$22^1/2$	
	2	Supports	2x6	$1^1/2$	$5^1/2$	7	Cut across diagonal for two pieces

Hardware

		Galvanized Deck Screws					
	2	Hanging Brackets					

Supplies

		Waterproof Glue					

REQUIRED TOOLS

Table or circular saw

Jigsaw, saber saw or band saw

Combination square

Drill

Hammer

Nail set

Screwdriver

Sander (or sandpaper and block)

Steel straightedge

Clamps

Measuring tape

1 Use waterproof glue and galvanized deck screws to build the box.

2 You can use clamps to hold the pieces in position while you build.

Construction Steps

Cut all the pieces to length as per the materials list. Using waterproof glue and galvanized deck screws, fasten the front of the box to the two ends. I used a waterproof yellow glue for this project, but one of the polyurethane types of adhesive might have been a better choice because it utilizes moisture in its curing process (see photos 1 and 2). Fasten the bottom to the inside of the box using glue and screws, then set the box aside until the glue has fully cured. Then, fasten the back to the bottom and two ends.

Use a ½" or ¾" spade bit to drill three or four drain holes in the bottom of the box (see photo 3).

Lay out the shapes of the support brackets, as you see I've done in the photographs. These do not need to be geometrically accurate. Any shape that pleases you will work well. I'm a great believer in the versatilities of the coffee can, which is what I use to lay out mine; you can do it freehand, if you like (see photos 4, 5 and 6).

3 Drill drain holes in the bottom of the box. You can use a spade bit to do this; size is not important.

4 To make the brackets, first mark out the piece just as you see in the drawing on page 63. Use the versatile coffee can to make the curves, or you can use a compass.

5 Here's how the piece should look once you've finished marking it out.

6 This is what should remain when you've finished the cutting.

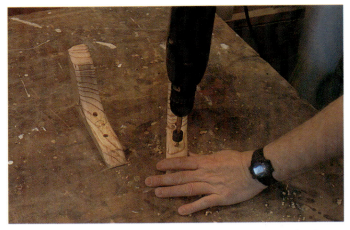

7 Use a ⅜" bit with a stop to partially drill the brackets for fastening screws.

8 Fasten the brackets to the bottom of the box, from the inside, using galvanized deck screws.

Use a ⅜" drill bit to counterbore two holes in the brackets. These will receive the screws that will fasten the box to the wall. Be careful not to counterbore too deep (see photo 7).

Drill ⅛" pilot holes through the counterbores. Using galvanized deck screws and glue, attach the brackets to the bottom of the box (see photo 8).

You have many finishing options with this piece. You can stain it and then apply a couple of coats of satin polyurethane, or you can prime and paint it with a couple of coats of outdoor-rated top coat in the color of your choice. All that then remains is to fasten on a couple of metal hanging brackets to the top of the back and it's ready to hang.

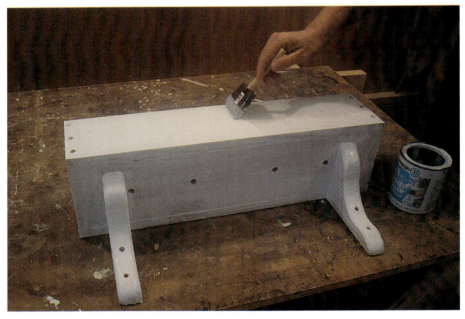

9 If you decide to paint your piece, apply a coat of stain-blocking primer before you apply the color coats.

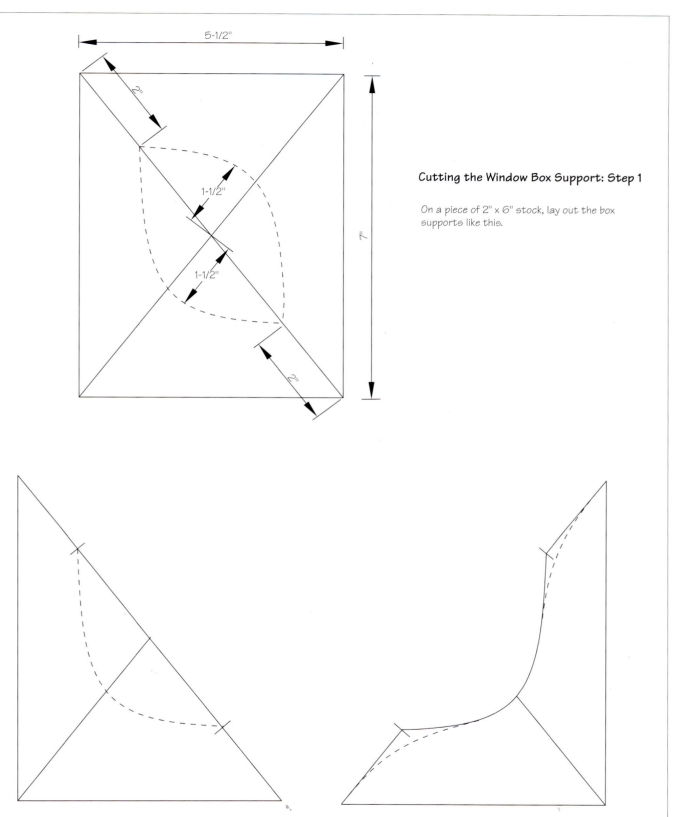

Cutting the Window Box Support: Step 1

On a piece of 2" x 6" stock, lay out the box supports like this.

Cutting the Window Box Support: Step 2

After making the layout, split the piece into two sections, and cut the basic curve.

Cutting the Window Box Support: Step 3

Having cut the basic curve, round out the sharp corners.

10

Small **Sideboard**

Sideboards make a nice addition to any room of the house. Though this piece is relatively small as sideboards go, it is large enough to display a range of ornaments without seeming too overcrowded. With the exception of some ripping and the assembly of the drawers, construction is fairly straight-forward. Each leg is constructed from two pieces of stock butt-jointed to-gether along one edge. Both the top and shelf are made from two pieces of stock edgejoint-ed together. The front part of the apron is made from five pieces of stock-size lumber, and the apron itself is glued and screwed to the legs.

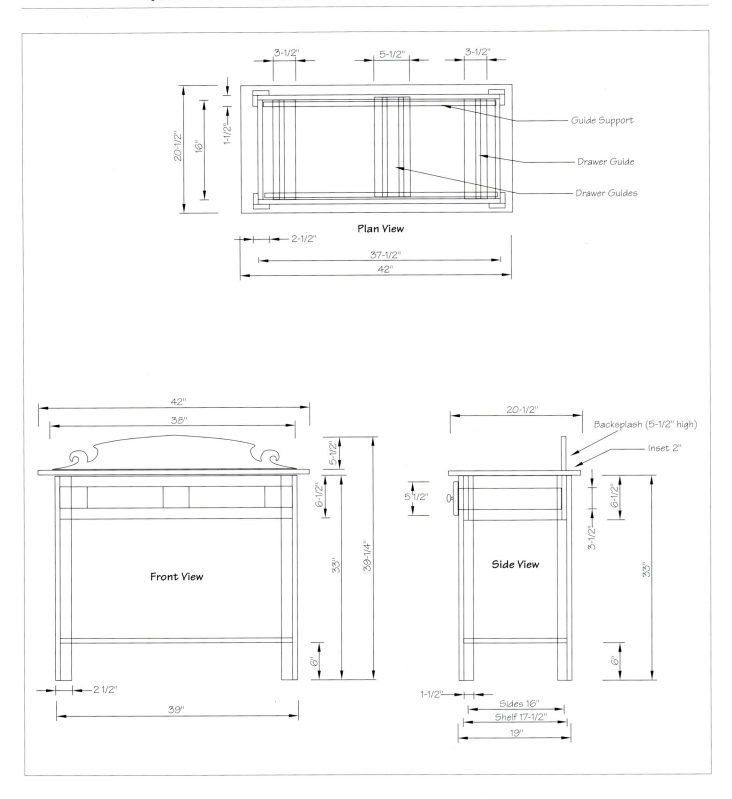

Plan View

Guide Support

Drawer Guide

Drawer Guides

Front View

Side View

Backsplash (5-1/2" high)

Inset 2"

Cutting List • Small Sideboard

REF.	QTY.	PART	STOCK	THICK	WIDTH	LENGTH	COMMENTS
	4	Legs	1x3	$3/4$	$2\frac{1}{2}$	33	
	4	Legs	1x2	$3/4$	$1\frac{1}{2}$	33	
	2	Apron Fronts	1x2	$3/4$	$1\frac{1}{2}$	$37\frac{1}{2}$	
	3	Apron Fronts	1x4	$3/4$	$3\frac{1}{2}$	4	
	2	Apron Sides	1x8	$3/4$	$7\frac{1}{4}$	16	
	1	Apron Back	1x8	$3/4$	$7\frac{1}{4}$	$37\frac{1}{2}$	
	1	Work Top	1x12	$3/4$	$20\frac{1}{2}$	42	Edge-join stock and rip to width
	1	Shelf	1x10	$3/4$	$17\frac{1}{2}$	$37\frac{1}{2}$	Edge-join stock and rip to width
	1	Backsplash	1x6	$3/4$	$5\frac{1}{2}$	38	
	2	Drawer Guide Supports	1x12	$3/4$	1	36	
	2	Outer Drawer Guides	1x4	$3/4$	$3\frac{1}{2}$	16	
	1	Central Drawer Guide	1x4	$3/4$	$5\frac{1}{2}$	16	
	4	Drawer Guides	1x2	$3/4$	$1\frac{1}{2}$	16	
	2	Drawer Fronts	1x4	$3/4$	$3\frac{1}{2}$	$11\frac{1}{8}$	
	2	Drawer Faces	1x6	$3/4$	$5\frac{1}{2}$	14	
	4	Drawer Sides	1x4	$3/4$	$3\frac{1}{2}$	$16\frac{1}{2}$	
	2	Drawer Backs	1x4	$3/4$	$2\frac{3}{4}$	$11\frac{1}{8}$	
	2	Drawer Bottoms	Plywood	$1/4$	$11\frac{5}{8}$	16	
	3	Cleats	1x4	$3/4$	$3\frac{1}{2}$	16	
	4	Shelf Supports	1x2	$3/4$	$1\frac{1}{2}$	6	

Hardware

REF.	QTY.	PART	STOCK	THICK	WIDTH	LENGTH	COMMENTS
		Drywall screws	No. 6			$1\frac{1}{4}$	
		Brads					
	2	Drawer Knobs					

Supplies

REF.	QTY.	PART	STOCK	THICK	WIDTH	LENGTH	COMMENTS
		Carpenter's Glue					

REQUIRED TOOLS

Table or circular saw

Jigsaw, saber saw or band saw

T-square jig

Drill

Hammer

Nail set

Screwdriver

Sander (or sandpaper block)

Measuring tape

Steel straightedge

Clamps

Chisel

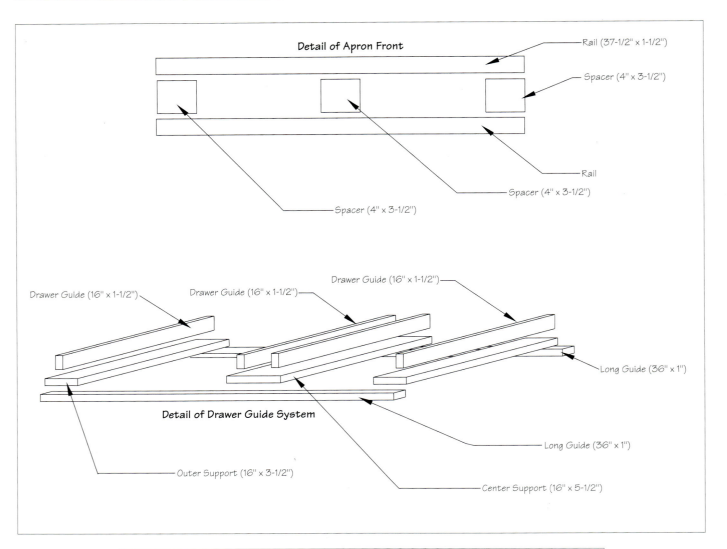

Detail of Apron Front

Rail (37-1/2" x 1-1/2")

Spacer (4" x 3-1/2")

Rail

Spacer (4" x 3-1/2")

Spacer (4" x 3-1/2")

Drawer Guide (16" x 1-1/2")

Drawer Guide (16" x 1-1/2")

Drawer Guide (16" x 1-1/2")

Long Guide (36" x 1")

Detail of Drawer Guide System

Long Guide (36" x 1")

Outer Support (16" x 3-1/2")

Center Support (16" x 5-1/2")

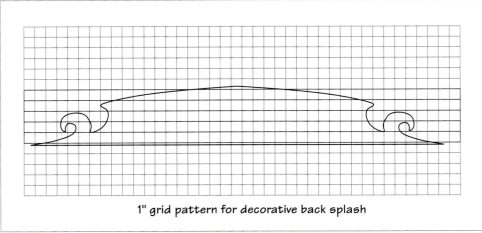

1" grid pattern for decorative back splash

Construction Steps

Cut the pieces for the top and shelf roughly to length as indicated in the materials list. Be very careful when you select the pieces for the top and shelf. These should be straight and true with no twists or warps. Edge-glue the pieces together that will form the top and shelf, clamp and then set them aside until the glue has fully cured, preferably overnight.

Take the five pieces that will form the front of the apron and lay out the position of each piece, then glue, clamp and set them aside until the glue has fully cured (see photo 1).

Take the eight pieces that will form the legs and lay them out on the bench. You should make sure you have two left-hand and two right-hand legs. That means you should lay the pieces out so that you have the joints facing the ends and a clear piece of stock for the front of each leg (see photos 2 and 3). Now glue and clamp the leg sections together. If you like, reinforce the joints with finishing nails.

1 Take the five pieces that will form the front section of the apron and lay them on the bench. Use glue and clamps to assemble them. When the glue has fully cured, sand the outer surface smooth.

2 Use eight pieces of stock, some glue, and some clamps to build the four legs.

3 When the glue has fully cured, remove the clamps and sand the legs smooth.

4 Use glue and drywall screws to build the apron: the five-piece front, the two ends, and the back panel.

5 You'll need to construct the board that will be used to make the lower shelf. Use glue and edge-joint the two pieces together. Clamp the pieces lightly; do not apply too much pressure—just enough to squeeze out a little glue—otherwise, the joint will be starved of glue and might fail.

Remove the clamps from the front section of the apron and set it on the bench along with the other three pieces of the apron. Build the apron box, gluing the butt joints, and reinforcing each joint with a couple of number 6×1¼" drywall screws (see photo 4). Measure the diagonals to ensure the box is square, and then set the structure aside until the glue has fully cured.

Trim the ends and rip down the width of the shelf so that it exactly matches the length and width of the apron box (see photo 5).

Remove the clamps from the apron box and, using some glue and drywall screws, from the inside, fasten the legs in position at the corners (see photo 6). When dry, stand the structure upright on the bench and glue and clamp the shelf supports in position at the bottom of the legs. These should be set against the back and front of each leg to make them unobtrusive once the piece is complete (see photo 7).

When everything has cured, apply a little glue to both the tops of the supports and the corners of the shelf. Then set the shelf in place on top of the supports. Clamp the legs to the shelf and the shelf to the tops of the supports, and set it aside until the glue has fully cured. You can reinforce each corner with a finishing nail, if you like,

6 Apply a little glue to the top inside five" of each of the legs. Use 1¼" drywall screws to fasten each leg in place on the outside of the apron, making sure the tops of the legs are flush with the top of the apron.

but it's not necessary (see photo 8).

Lay the structure facedown on the bench with the open top facing toward you. Using some glue and drywall screws, fasten one of the drawer guide supports to the bottom of the inside of the front of the apron (see photo 9). Turn the structure over and repeat the process, fastening the other drawer guide support to the bottom inside of the back.

7 Stand the leg/apron structure upright on the bench and glue the shelf supports in place at the bottom of each leg.

8 Set the shelf in position on top of the supports. Make sure the shelf fits tightly into each corner. You might need to use clamps to pull them together.

9 Fasten the drawer support rails in position using glue and screws.

Set the structure on its feet and, using some glue and drywall screws, build the drawer guides and supports as you see them in the drawing (see photos 10, 11, 12 and 13). Apply a little glue to the drawer guide supports inside the apron and set the drawer guides in place, making sure they are square and in line with the outer edges of the drawer openings; fasten them down with drywall screws.

Take two of the three cleats that will be used to fasten the top to the understructure and, using a little glue, set them in place at the top and ends of the apron opening. Clamp them in position and let the glue cure overnight. Then take the third cleat, apply glue to its ends, and set it in place at the center and top of the opening. Fasten it in place with a couple of brads, back and front, apply a clamp and let dry.

At this point you'll need to finish working the backsplash/rail. First, make a pattern of the detail and mark out the two ends of the rail. Use your jigsaw to cut out the detail. Take your time, do the job in small bights, and move the saw just a little bit at a time around the tight curves. Sand all the inside and outside edges of the details and smooth away the sharp edges. Finish-sand both the top and the backsplash prior to fastening them together.

Apply a little glue to the lower edge of the backsplash, and then set it carefully in place on the top. From the rear, apply two or three clamps; don't overtighten them. Apply just enough pressure to squeeze a little glue out of the joint, then leave it overnight or until the glue has fully cured.

Set the top in position on top of the understructure and hold it in place with three or four clamps. From the underside, fasten the top, through the cleats, to the understructure using three drywall screws at each end and three more at the center.

Now it's time to build the drawers. Take the two pieces that will form the false fronts and, using your circular saw and T-square jig, cut the rabbets at each end. Use a straightedge and your circular saw to cut the slot along the

10 Fasten the center drawer support in position on the rails using glue and screws.

11 Fasten the end drawer supports in position on the rails using glue and screws.

bottoms of the two false fronts and four sides that will receive the plywood bottoms. The slot should be ¼" deep and ¼" wide, which means you'll need to make two cuts down the grain side by side. Not a difficult task, if you take your time.

Use a little glue in the rabbets and fasten the drawer sides to the false fronts using two 1¼" drywall screws at each joint. Set the drawer backs in po-

sition—no need to use any glue—and fasten them in position using two 1¼" drywall screws at each joint. Try the drawers in their slots to make sure they slide in and out freely. If not, you'll need to make some adjustments.

Finish-sand the two real drawer fronts, smooth off the sharp edges, then set them facedown on the bench. Apply a little glue to the back of one of the drawer fronts, then set its drawer in place, the false to the back of the real front, then fasten it in place with a couple of drywall screws. Repeat the process for the second of the two drawers, making sure that the two real fronts are properly in line with each other. Then slide the plywood drawer bottoms into their slots and fasten them with a couple of small nails along the back of the drawers. There's no need to nail the sides.

Fasten the knobs in place and then sand all the outer surfaces smooth. Start with 80-grit sandpaper and finish with 150-grit; as soft as the pine is, anything finer would be just a waste of time. Make sure you remove all the tool marks. To finish the piece, you can either paint it or stain it, as I have, then apply a couple of coats of polyurethane to protect it.

12 Fasten the center drawer guide in position on the support using glue and screws.

13 Fasten the end drawer guides in position on the supports using glue and screws. Make sure all guides are square with the front openings. If not, the drawer will either be a sloppy fit or will bind.

11

Adirondack
Chair

The Adirondack chair is not only aesthetically pleasing, it's comfortable and therapeutic. You only have to sit in one to see what I mean. I've used pressure-treated pine for this project, since it comes in stock sizes and is rot resistant. You could use other wood, such as cedar, teak or cypress, but if you do, be prepared to do some extra work, as they don't come in stock sizes. Construction is achieved using carriage bolts and screws for strength. Assembly is quite simple, and you can either leave the chair natural or paint it. If you do paint it, use a stain-blocking primer before applying the finishing coats.

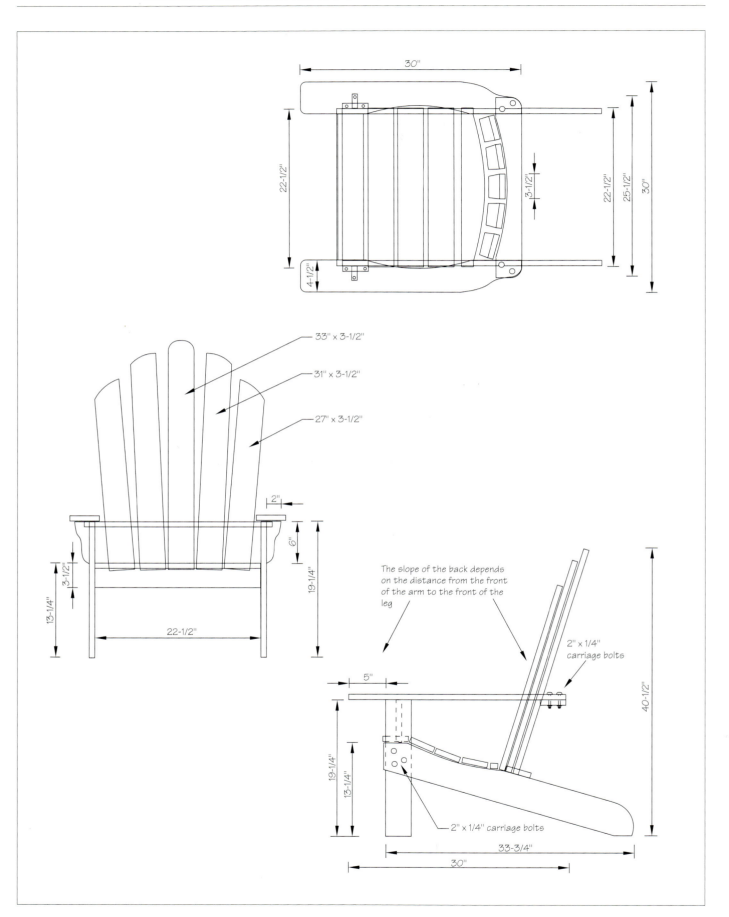

33" x 3-1/2"

31" x 3-1/2"

27" x 3-1/2"

The slope of the back depends on the distance from the front of the arm to the front of the leg

2" x 1/4" carriage bolts

2" x 1/4" carriage bolts

Cutting List • Adirondack Chair

REF.	QTY.	PART	STOCK	THICK	WIDTH	LENGTH	COMMENTS
	2	Back Legs	1x6	$3/4$	$4^1/_2$	36	Use pressure-treated lumber
	2	Front Legs	1x4	$3/4$	$3^1/_2$	$19^1/_4$	
	2	Arms	1x6	$3/4$	$4^1/_2$	30	
	1	Hip and First Seat Slat	1x6	$3/4$	$5^1/_2$	$22^1/_2$	
	1	Seat Rail	1x4	$3/4$	$3^1/_2$	$22^1/_2$	
	1	Shoulder	1x4	$3/4$	$3^1/_2$	$25^1/_2$	
	4	Seat Slats	1x4	$3/4$	$3^1/_2$	$22^1/_2$	
	1	Center Splat	1x4	$3/4$	$3^1/_2$	33	
	2	Second Splats	1x4	$3/4$	$3^1/_2$	31	
	2	Third Splats	1x4	$3/4$	$3^1/_2$	27	
	2	Arm Supports	1x4	$3/4$	2	6	

Hardware

REF.	QTY.	PART	STOCK	THICK	WIDTH	LENGTH	COMMENTS
	10	Carriage Bolts		$1/4$		2	
		Galvanized Deck Screws				$1^3/_4$	

Supplies

REF.	QTY.	PART	STOCK	THICK	WIDTH	LENGTH	COMMENTS
		Waterproof Glue					

REQUIRED TOOLS

Table or circular saw

Combination square

Drill

Screwdriver

Jigsaw or band saw

Measuring tape

Sander(or sandpaper and block)

Steel straightedge

Clamps

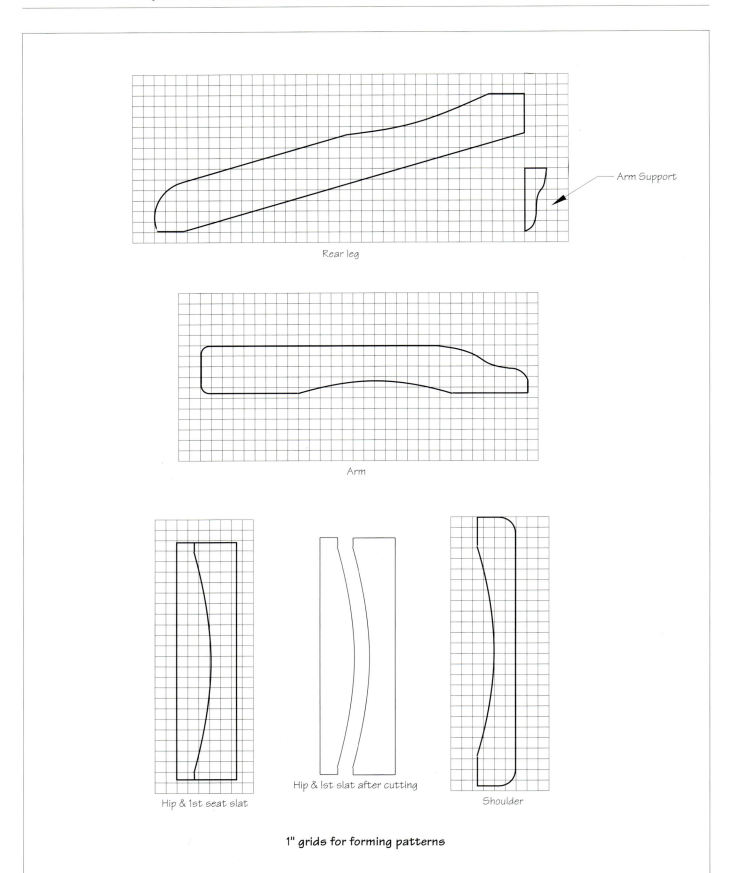

Arm Support

Rear leg

Arm

Hip & 1st seat slat

Hip & !st slat after cutting

Shoulder

1" grids for forming patterns

1 After you've cut all of your pieces roughly to length, you'll need to make patterns, then use these to mark out the arms and rear legs.

2 You'll also need patterns to make the hip and first seat slat and the shoulder.

Construction Steps

The first step is to make plywood templates of each of the seven shaped sections—arms, back legs, hip and first seat slat, the ends of the splats and the arm supports. That way, once your family and friends see how comfortable this chair is, it will be easy to go back and make more. Simply lay out the shapes, cut them out with your jigsaw, and then take off the rough edges with some sandpaper.

Cut all the pieces to length and, using your plywood patterns, mark out the shaped sections. Use the same pattern you used for the hip and first seat slat to mark the shoulder. Just center the pattern on the stock before you make your mark (see photos 1 and 2). With your jigsaw, cut the shaped arms, back legs and the ends of the splats. Then tilt the base of the jigsaw to 13° and cut the hip and first seat slat from the single piece of 1×6 stock (see photo 3). Then tilt the jigsaw base to about 26° and cut the curve to the shoulder section (see photo 4).

3 After you've marked out the hip and first seat lat and the shoulder, you'll need to set your jigsaw to cut at an angle of roughly 26° to cut out the shoulder and 13° to cut out the hip and first seat slat.

4 It's best if you clamp the two arm and two rear leg sections together before you use your jigsaw to cut out the shapes—the cutout from the arm makes the underarm support.

5 Set one front leg on the bench; set one rear leg on top of it, with a little waterproof glue in between, and drill the three holes to receive the carriage bolts.

6 Lay both leg sections against the bench and set the seat rail in position on the front of each and secure it with galvanized deck screws.

Lay one of the back legs on the bench, outer side up, and then lay the front leg in position on top of it (see photo 5). Drill the three holes for the carriage bolts that will fasten the two legs together. Separate the two legs, apply a little waterproof glue around the holes, put them back together and drive the carriage bolts through the holes. Turn the structure over, add washers to the ends of the bolts, and tighten the nuts. Repeat the process for the second pair of legs, making sure that the second unit is a mirror image of the first.

Set the shoulder section on the bench, then set the two arms in position on top of it. Drill the four ¼" holes that will receive the carriage bolts that fasten the three pieces together. Remove the arms, apply glue around the holes, set the arms back in position and drive the carriage bolts through the holes. Turn the structure over, add washers and tighten.

Lay the two leg sections against the bench and set the seat rail in position on the ends of the back legs (see photo 6). Using 1¾" galvanized deck screws, fasten the seat rail in position, making sure it's square with the ends of the back legs (see photo 7). Set the resulting structure on the bench and fasten the supports onto the front legs with deck screws. Now fasten the hip in position on top of the two back legs (see photo 8).

7 Use two screws at each end of the seat rail and make sure the resulting structure is square and true.

8 Set the hip in position at the end of the curved cuts on the two rear legs and secure it in position with galvanized deck screws, two to each joint.

9 Set the shoulder on the bench and one arm on top of one end, with a little waterproof glue between them. Make sure they form a perfect right angle, then drill holes for the two carriage bolts that will secure the two pieces together. Repeat the process at the other end, using the second arm.

10 Fasten the arm supports in position and set the arm structure on top of the chair base (the end of the arm should be roughly 5" forward from the upright leg). Fasten the arms to the tops of the legs and the supports using galvanized deck screws.

Cut two pieces of scrap to exactly the same length as the front legs (19¼"). Set the arm section in position on top of the front legs and use the two pieces of scrap stock as a prop to hold up the back of the leg section (see photo 9). Measure the distance from the front of each arm to the front of each front leg (it should be 5"), then fasten the arms in place using three deck screws to each arm—one in the support and two into the top of the leg (see photo 10). Remove the props; the arms will now support themselves.

Set the center back splat in position. Make sure it's exactly in the middle and fasten it in position with a single screw (see photo 11). Use a square to make sure the splat is upright, then complete the installation with a couple more screws—one at the bottom and one more at the shoulder. Then fasten the other four splats in position.

Take the first seat slat—the one you cut from the hip and first section—and use screws to fasten it in position against the bottom of the splats (see photo 12). Set the remaining seat slats in place and fasten them down with screws. The assembly is now complete (see photo 13).

11 Fasten the center back splat to the middle of the shoulder using just one screw. Make sure the splat is perfectly upright and secure it to the hip using one screw at the center. Then fasten the rest of the splats in position on the hip and shoulder, using three screws per splat—two at the shoulder, one at the hip.

12 Fasten the first shaped seat slat in position using one screw at each end. Then fasten the rest of the seat slats in position to complete the chair.

12

Adirondack
Table

This attractive table makes a great companion piece to the chair from the previous chapter. This is a very simple piece to build. The main thing you have to keep in mind is to make sure the legs are all exactly the same length and that the two leg/stretcher sections are perfectly square. The rest, as they say, is simply a matter of hanging it all together.

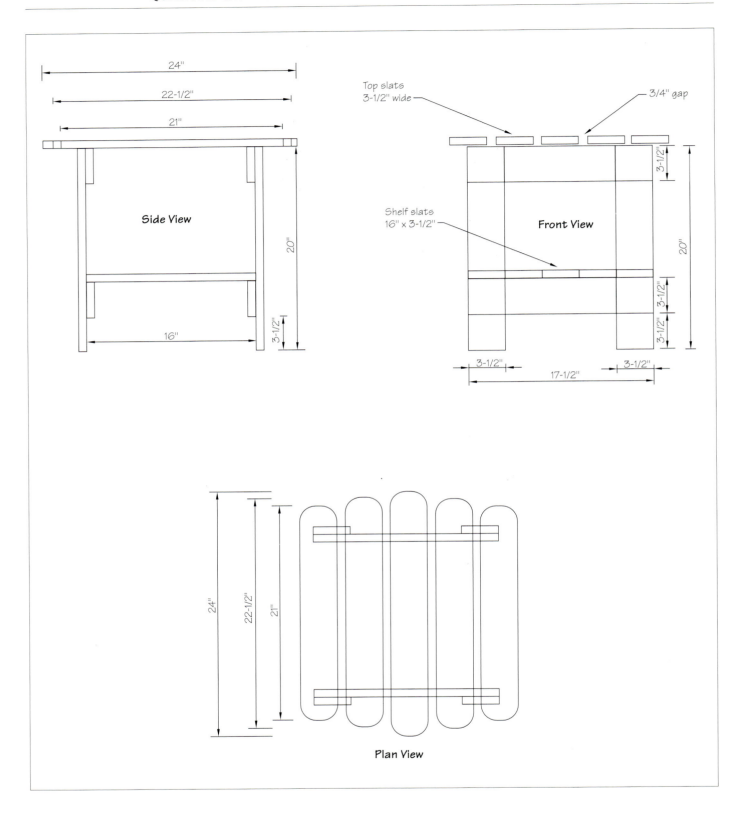

24"

22-1/2"

21"

Side View

20"

16"

3-1/2"

Top slats
3-1/2" wide

3/4" gap

3-1/2"

Shelf slats
16" x 3-1/2"

Front View

20"

3-1/2"

3-1/2"

3-1/2"

17-1/2"

3-1/2"

24"

22-1/2"

21"

Plan View

Cutting List • Adirondack Table

REF.	QTY.	PART	STOCK	THICK	WIDTH	LENGTH	COMMENTS
	4	Legs	1x6	3/4	3½	20	Use pressure-treated lumber
	5	Shelf Boards	1x6	3/4	3½	16	
	4	Stretchers	1x6	3/4	3½	17½	
	1	Top	1x6	3/4	3½	24	
	2	Tops	1x6	3/4	3½	22½	
	2	Tops	1x6	3/4	3½	21	

Hardware

		Galvanized Deck Screws				1¼	

Supplies

		Waterproof Glue					

REQUIRED TOOLS

Table or circular saw

Combination square

Drill

Screwdriver

Jigsaw, saber saw or bandsaw

Measuring tape

Sander (or sandpaper and block)

Steel straightedge

Clamps

Construction Steps

Cut all of the pieces exactly to length as indicated in the materials list. With a coffee can and your jigsaw, round the ends of the five pieces that make up the top (see photos 1, 2 and 3).

Set two legs on the bench, then set two stretchers in position on the legs. Make note of exactly where they are and then remove them (see photo 4). Apply a little waterproof glue and reposition the stretchers. Use one screw at each joint to secure the stretchers to the legs; don't use more than one screw at each joint because you need to be able to move the pieces to square them up (see photo 5). Measure the diagonal, or use a setsquare, to ensure the leg section is true and square. When you are sure the structure is absolutely square, use four more screws to firmly secure each joint. Repeat these steps to build the second leg section.

1 Use the good old coffee can to mark out the curved ends of the boards that will form the tabletop.

2 Use your jigsaw to cut the ends of the tabletop pieces.

3 If you have a router, round over the edges of the boards that will form the tabletop. If not, you can take off the edges with sandpaper.

4 Having cut all the pieces to length, set two of the shorter stretchers in place on two of the legs.

5 Fasten the stretchers to the legs using galvanized deck screws.

Stand the two leg sections on their feet, the stretchers facing inward. Set one shelf board in position between the two leg sections, flush with the edge, and secure it in place with a couple of deck screws at each end (see photo 6). Set the rest of the leg sections in place and secure them with deck screws.

Use your square to ensure the leg sections are at right angles to the shelf, then set the longest of the boards that will form the top in position in the center and on top of the two leg sections. Now fasten it in place with four deck screws: two at each end and into the tops of the leg sections (see photo 7). Repeat the process for the remaining four top boards (see photo 8). Then all that remains is to either leave the piece in its natural state, or finish it off with a couple of coats of exterior primer and a couple more of exterior paint in the color of your choice.

6 Set one of the shelf boards in place between the two legs sections, level with the edge of the stretchers, and secure it in place with galvanized deck screws. Then fasten the other four boards in place to complete the shelf.

7 Set the center top board in position in the middle of the top of the frame. Measure to make sure that the piece is centered and that the overhang is the same on either side. Fasten it in position using galvanized deck screws.

8 Set the other four top sections in place; use a small stick to make sure the gaps between the boards are all the same.

Stains

STAIN TYPE	FORM	PREPARATION	CHARACTERISTICS
Pigment stains			
Oil-based	Liquid	Mix thoroughly	Apply with rag, brush or spray; resists fading.
Water-based	Liquid	Mix thoroughly	Apply with rag, brush or spray; resists fading; water cleanup.
Gel	Gel	Ready to use	Apply with rag; won't raise grain; easy to use; no drips or runs.
Water-based gel	Gel	Ready to use	Apply with rag; easy to use; no drips or runs.
Japan color	Concentrated liquid	Mix thoroughly	Used for tinting stains, paints, varnish, lacquer.
Dye stains			
Water-based	Powder	Mix with water	Apply with rag, brush or spray; deep penetrating; best resistance of dye stains; good clarity; raises grain.
Oil-based	Powder	Mix with toluol, lacquer thinner, turpentine or naphtha	Apply with rag, brush or spray; penetrating; does not raise grain; dries slowly.
Alcohol-based	Powder	Mix with alcohol	Apply with rag, brush or spray; penetrating; does not raise grain; dries quickly; lap marks sometimes a problem.
NGR	Liquid	Mix thoroughly	Apply with rag, brush or spray (use retarder if wiping or brushing); good clarity; does not raise grain.

Topcoats

FINISH TYPE	FORM	PREPARATION	CHARACTERISTICS	DRY TIME
Shellac	Liquid	Mix thoroughly	Dries quickly; economical; available either clear or amber-colored; high gloss luster; affected by water, alcohol and heat.	2 hours
Shellac flakes	Dry flakes	Mix with alcohol	Dries quickly; economical (mix only what is needed); color choices from amber to clear; high gloss luster; affected by water, alcohol and heat.	2 hours
Lacquer	Liquid	Mix with thinner for spraying	Dries quickly; clear (shaded lacquers available); high gloss luster, but flattening agents available; durable; moisture resistant.	30 minutes
Varnish	Liquid	Mix thoroughly	Dries slowly; amber color; gloss, semi-gloss and satin lusters; very good durability and moisture resistance; flexible.	3 to 6 hours
Polyurethane	Liquid	Mix thoroughly	Dries slowly; clear to amber colors; gloss, semi-gloss and satin lusters; excellent durability and moisture resistance; flexible.	3 to 6 hours
Water-based polyurethane	Liquid	Mix thoroughly	Dries quickly; clear; won't yellow; gloss and satin lusters; moisture and alcohol resistant; low odor.	2 hours
Tung oil	Liquid	Ready to use	Dries slowly; amber color; satin luster; poor moisture resistance; easy to use.	20 to 24 hours
Danish oil	Liquid	Mix thoroughly	Dries slowly; amber color; satin luster; poor moisture resistance; easy to use.	8 to 10 hours

NOTE: Dry times are based on a temperature of 70° Fahrenheit and 40 percent relative humidity. Lower temperature and/or higher relative humidity can increase drying time.

13

Adirondack
Ottoman

The ottoman effectively turns the Adirondack chair into a lounger. The design of this one elongates and accentuates the classic lines of the chair. If you've never sat in one of these chair/ottoman combinations, you're in for a treat. There's nothing quite like relaxing in the cool morning sunshine with a good book and a glass of iced tea; it's about as close to Utopia as you can get.

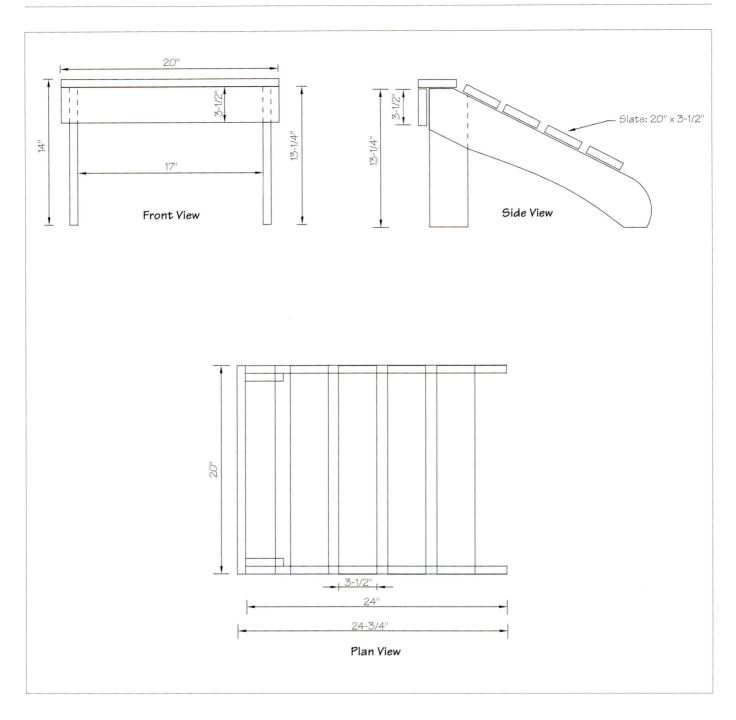

20"

3-1/2"

14"

13-1/4"

17"

Front View

3-1/2"

13-1/4"

Slats: 20" x 3-1/2"

Side View

20"

3-1/2"

24"

24-3/4"

Plan View

Cutting List • Adirondack Ottoman

REF.	QTY.	PART	STOCK	THICK	WIDTH	LENGTH	COMMENTS
	2	Sides	1x6	$3/4$	$5\frac{1}{2}$	24	Use pressure treated lumber
	2	Legs	1x6	$3/4$	$3\frac{1}{2}$	$13\frac{1}{4}$	
	1	Front Rail	1x6	$3/4$	$3\frac{1}{2}$	20	
	5	Slats	1x6	$3/4$	$3\frac{1}{2}$	20	

Hardware

		Galvanized deck screws					

REQUIRED TOOLS

Table or circular saw

Drill

Screwdriver

Jigsaw or bandsaw

Measuring Tape

Straight edge

Clamps

Construction Steps

Cut all the pieces to length as per the materials list. Lay out the shapes on the two side sections. These do not have to be geometrically accurate. I laid mine out by freehand, then used the first piece to make a plywood template. You'll need to do so too; once you see how comfortable this ottoman and chair combination are, there's no doubt that you'll be making more than one set (see photo 1, 2 &3).

Using galvanized deck screws attach the legs to the sides. Make sure that you make them as mirror images of each other. There should be a left and a right (see photo 4). Now fasten the front rail, first to the front of one of the two side sections, then to the other (see photo 5).

Stand the resulting structure upright on the bench and attach the slats to the top, make sure the spacing between each piece is equal (see photo 6). Do any necessary sanding and either leave the piece in its natural state, or apply the finish of your choice.

1 Make a template to mark out the detail for the side sections. This way you can be sure you can repeat the process if you make more than one ottoman.

2 Use your jigsaw to cut out the sides. Be sure to raise the piece up off the bench.

3 If you have a router, round the edges of the sides. If not, you can ease the edges with a sander or sandpaper.

4 Apply a little waterproof glue, then set the leg in place on the inside of the side section; drill pilot holes for the screws. Use galvanized deck screws to secure the leg to the side section.

5 Fasten the front rail to one of the leg/side sections using galvanized deck screws.

6 Fasten the slats in place using galvanized deck screws.

14

Picket
Planter

The great thing about this attractive little planter is that not only is it functional, it can be made almost entirely from scrap and offcuts. It can be made from pressure-treated or regular framing lumber and can be stained, painted or, if you do decide to make it from pressure-treated material, left to age naturally in the outdoors. As it's made from stock sizes, there is no ripping to do. Construction is achieved using finishing nails and screws and can be completed easily in an afternoon. The top has a recess for a potted plant, while a door hides a cavity beneath the upper shelf where you can store tools, soil, etc.

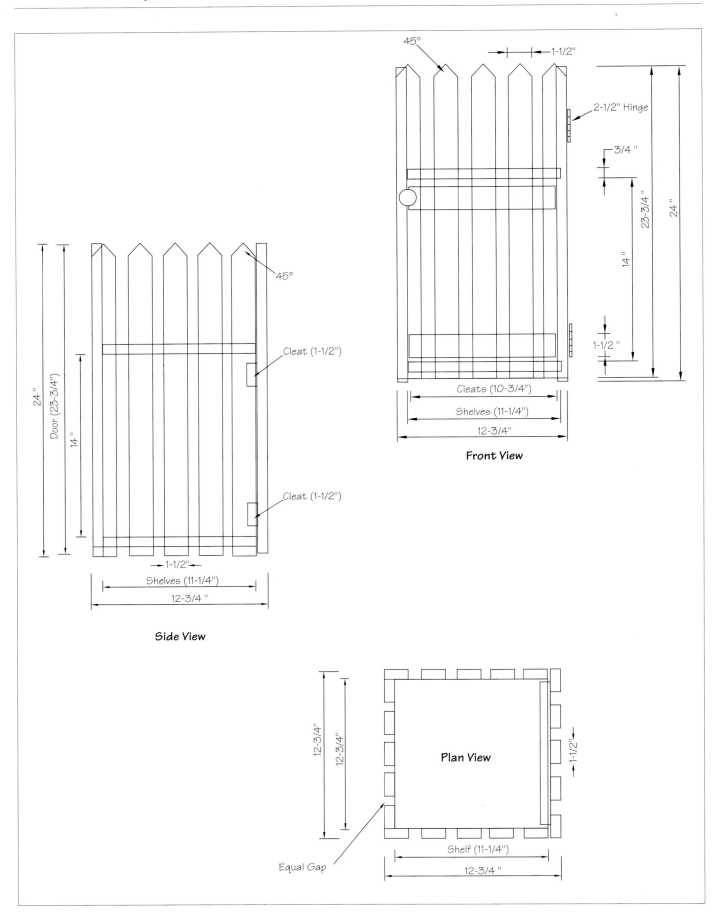

45°

1-1/2"

2-1/2" Hinge

3/4"

23-3/4"

14"

24"

1-1/2"

Cleats (10-3/4")

Shelves (11-1/4")

12-3/4"

Front View

45°

Cleat (1-1/2")

Cleat (1-1/2")

24"

Door (23-3/4")

14"

1-1/2"

Shelves (11-1/4")

12-3/4"

Side View

12-3/4"

12-3/4"

1-1/2"

Plan View

Equal Gap

Shelf (11-1/4")

12-3/4"

Cutting List • Picket Planter

REF.	QTY.	PART	STOCK	THICK	WIDTH	LENGTH	COMMENTS
	2	Shelves	1x12	$3/4$	$11^{1}/_{4}$	$11^{1}/_{4}$	
	15	Pickets	1x2	$3/4$	$1^{1}/_{2}$	24	
	5	Door Pickets	1x2	$3/4$	$1^{1}/_{2}$	$23^{3}/_{4}$	
	2	Cleats	1x2	$3/4$	$1^{1}/_{2}$	11	

Hardware

	QTY.	PART	STOCK				
	2	Steel Hinges					
		Finishing Nails					
		Galvanized Screws	#6				

REQUIRED TOOLS

Table or circular saw

Jigsaw/saber saw, band saw

Drill

Sander (or sandpaper and block)

Screwdriver

Hammer

Nail set

Measuring tape

Steel straightedge

Clamps

Combination square

Construction Steps

Cut all of the pieces to length as per the materials list. If you're using pieces of scrap, trim the shelves to their finished dimensions. Use the 45° angle on your combination square to mark out the points on the ends of the pickets (see photo 1).

Stand the two shelves on edge about 14" apart, with the smooth edges up (both end grains should be showing). This will form the back of the planter. Set one of the pickets in place at one of the corners; use a small piece of stock to set the blunt end of the picket ¾" from the underside of the shelf. This will raise the lower shelf up off the floor (see photo 2).

Nail the bottom end of the picket in place; use one nail only at this point. Measure the distance between the two shelves (the upper shelf should be 14" above the lower shelf) and use one nail to fasten the picket in place (see photo 3). Use your square to true up the shelves and the picket, then use a second nail to set the lower shelf and another to set the upper shelf. You should now have two shelves fastened together at one corner by one picket.

1 Cut all the pieces roughly to length, then mark out the points using the 45° angle on your combination square.

2 Set the first picket in position on the lower shelf, secure it with a nail, make sure it's square, then fasten it securely in position using a second nail.

3 Set the upper section in position, measure for the correct distance, and then secure it with a nail. Make sure the shelf is square with the picket.

Take another picket and fasten it in place at the other corner on the same side as the first one, using the same small piece of stock to establish its position at the bottom of the planter (see photo 4). Then take three more pickets and set them in place between the first two. Use a straightedge to line them up along the bottom and a measuring tape to set the gaps equally between them (see photo 5). Nail everything carefully in place. Repeat the process for the two sides, making sure the shelves are square with the back. You should now have a complete planter, minus the door, with an opening at the front.

To build the door, set the planter upright on the bench, then stand the two cleats on the shelves in the front of the planter (see photo 6). Take one of the five remaining pickets and hold it in place against the front of the planter and carefully mark the position of the cleats.

4 Fasten the second picket in position at the other end of the lower shelf.

5 Fasten the other pickets in place between the first two pickets to complete the first side. Make sure the bottom is flush and that the pickets are equally spaced.

6 Begin to build the door by placing two of the pickets on the bench, and then placing the two cleats on top of them. Fasten them together using galvanized screws.

Remove the cleats from the planter and lay them on the bench in roughly the same position they will occupy in the planter. Set one of the pickets in place on the outer edge of the cleats and fasten it in place with a single screw to each cleat, allow room for a second screw when you're sure you have the pickets in the correct positions. Repeat the process, using a second picket at the other edge. You should now have something that looks like a frame.

Hold the frame against the opening in the planter, square it up and make sure it fits the hole. When you are sure the door fits the opening properly, add a second screw to each corner, thus setting the door so that the corners cannot move. Add the remaining three pickets (see photo 7), then set the door in place in the planter and turn it on its edge, hinge side up, on the bench. Fasten the hinges in place (see photo 8).

All that remains now is to finish the piece. If you decide to paint your planter, you'll need to give it a couple of coats of primer before you add the finishing coats. Be sure you use an outdoor-rated paint.

7 Complete the door by placing the rest of the pickets in position and then securing them with galvanized screws.

8 Fasten the door to the planter using two decorative hinges.

Metric Conversions

U.S. UNITS TO METRIC EQUIVALENTS			METRIC UNITS TO U.S. EQUIVALENTS		
To convert from	Multiply by	To get	To convert from	Multiply by	To get
Inches	25.4	Millimeters	Millimeters	0.0394	Inches
Inches	2.54	Centimeters	Centimeters	0.3937	Inches
Feet	30.48	Centimeters	Centimeters	0.0328	Feet
Feet	0.3048	Meters	Meters	3.2808	Feet
Yards	0.9144	Meters	Meters	1.0936	Yards
Square inches	6.4516	Square centimeters	Square centimeters	0.1550	Square inches
Square feet	0.0929	Square meters	Square meters	10.764	Square feet Square
yards	0.8361	Square meters	Square meters	1.1960	Square yards
Acres	0.4047	Hectares	Hectares	2.4711	Acres
Cubic inches	16.387	Cubic centimeters	Cubic centimeters	0.0610	Cubic inches
Cubic feet	0.0283	Cubic meters	Cubic meters	35.315	Cubic feet
Cubic feet	28.316	Liters	Liters	0.0353	Cubic feet
Cubic yards	0.7646	Cubic meters	Cubic meters	1.308	Cubic yards
Cubic yards	764.55	Liters	Liters	0.0013	Cubic yards
Ounces (fluid)	0.0296	Liters	Liters	33.784	Ounces (fluid)
Pints	0.4732	Liters	Liters	2.1133	Pints
Quarts	0.9464	Liters	Liters	1.0566	Quarts
Gallons	3.7854	Liters	Liters	0.2642	Gallons
Ounces (weight)	28.350	Grams	Grams	0.3527	Ounces (weight)
Pounds	0.4536	Kilograms	Kilograms	2.2046	Pounds

Lumber

WOOD SIZE (MILLIMETERS)	NEAREST U.S. EQUIVALENT (INCHES)
25 x 75	1 x 3
50 x 100	2 x 4
50 x 150	2 x 6
50 x 200	2 x 8
50 x 250	2 x 10
50 x 300	2 x 12

Fractions to Metric Equivalents

INCHES	MILLIMETERS	INCHES	MILLIMETERS	INCHES	MILLIMETERS	INCHES	MILLIMETERS
1/64	0.396875	17/64	6.746875	33/64	13.096880	49/64	19.446880
1/32	0.793750	9/32	7.143750	17/32	13.493750	25/32	19.843750
3/64	1.190625	19/64	7.540625	35/64	13.890630	51/64	20.240630
1/16	1.587500	5/16	7.937500	9/16	14.287500	13/16	20.637500
5/64	1.984375	21/64	8.334375	37/64	14.684380	53/64	21.034380
3/32	2.381250	11/32	8.731250	19/32	15.081250	27/32	21.431250
7/64	2.778125	23/64	9.128125	39/64	15.478130	55/64	21.828130
1/8	3.175000	3/8	9.525000	5/8	15.875000	7/8	22.225000
9/64	3.571875	25/64	9.921875	41/64	16.271880	57/64	22.621880
5/32	3.968750	13/32	10.318750	21/32	16.668750	29/32	23.018750
11/64	4.365625	27/64	10.715630	43/64	17.065630	59/64	23.415630
3/16	4.762500	7/16	11.112500	11/16	17.462500	15/16	23.812500
13/64	5.159375	29/64	11.509380	45/64	17.859380	61/64	24.209380
7/32	5.556250	15/32	11.906250	23/32	18.256250	31/32	24.606250
15/64	5.953125	31/64	12.303130	47/64	18.653130	63/64	25.003130
1/4	6.350000	1/2	12.700000	3/4	19.050000	1	25.400000

15

Plate
Rack

Plate racks are practical, attractive and offer a convenient way to show off family heirlooms. These racks come in all sorts of shapes and sizes. This one, based on an old design I found in a library book, hangs in our dining room and is a great conversation piece. It's quite easy to build and can be completed over a weekend. It is built entirely from stock lumber, but you will need to rip two narrow pieces from one of the larger sizes. There are no plate grooves in this version; I've used narrow strips of wood instead. If you happen to own a router, you can do away with the strips in favor of grooves.

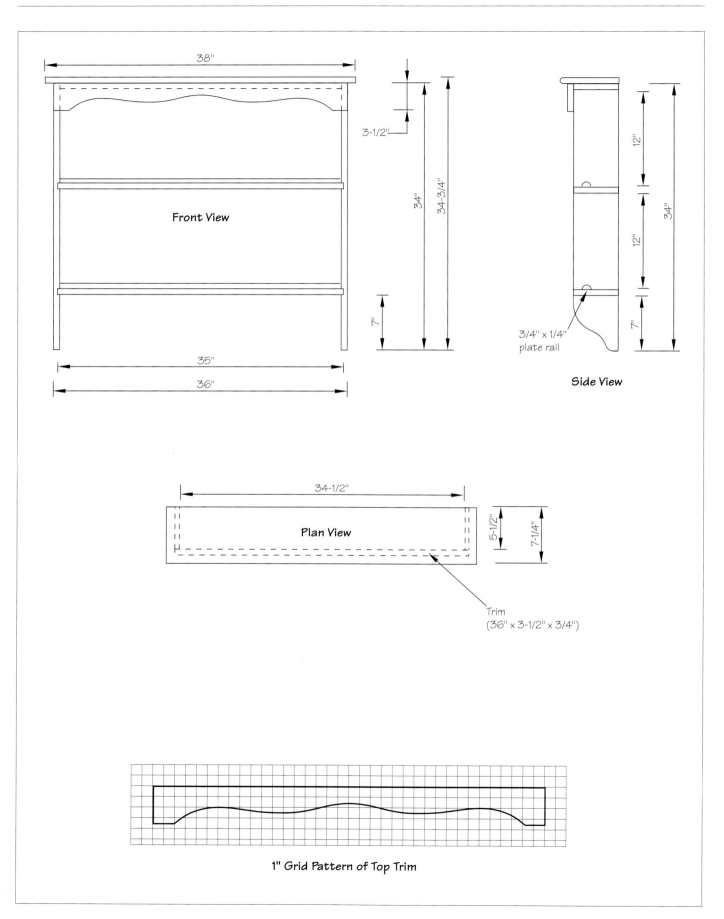

Front View

38"

3-1/2"

34"

34-3/4"

7"

35"

36"

Side View

12"

12"

34"

7"

3/4" x 1/4" plate rail

Plan View

34-1/2"

5-1/2"

7-1/4"

Trim
(36" x 3-1/2" x 3/4")

1" Grid Pattern of Top Trim

Cutting List • Plate Rack

REF.	QTY.	PART	STOCK	THICK	WIDTH	LENGTH	COMMENTS
	2	Sides	1 x 12	$^3/_4$	$5^1/_2$	34	
	3	Shelves	1 x 6	$^3/_4$	$5^1/_2$	35	
	1	Crown	1 x 8	$^3/_4$	$7^1/_2$	38	
	2	Strips	1 x 2	$^3/_4$	$^1/_4$	$34^1/_2$	
	1	Trim	1 x 4	$^3/_4$	$3^1/_2$	36	

Hardware

		Drywall Screws				$1^1/_4$	
		Brads				$^3/_4$	
	2	Hangers					

Supplies

		Carpenter's Glue					

REQUIRED TOOLS

Table or circular saw

Drill

Screwdriver

Jigsaw/saber saw or band saw

Sander (or sandpaper and block)

Measuring tape

Steel straightedge

Chisel

Clamps

T-square jig

Hammer

Nail set

Construction Steps

Cut all the pieces to length as per the materials list. To ensure that your side dadoes match exactly, cut the two side boards out of one piece of stock; you'll rip it into two pieces after you've milled the dadoes. Rip the two plate restraint strips to ¼" thick. Lay the two sides (still as one piece of lumber) inside up on the bench and mark the positions for the dadoes and rabbets.

Make a pattern from a small piece of ¼" plywood and mark out the details at the bottom of each of the two sides. Use your jigsaw to cut out the details, and then sand the two sides smooth, taking care to smooth the inside edges and to ease all the sharp edges (see photo 2).

Take the piece of 3½" stock that will form the trim and lay out the decorative detail. You can do this by finding the center of the piece, then marking one side by freehand. Cut this section out with your jigsaw and then use the offcut to mark out the other half (see photo 3). Finish cutting the trim detail, and then sand smooth.

1 Use a straight-edge, clamps and your circular saw to split the two sides apart.

2 After you've marked the cutouts at the bottom end of each of the two sides, use your jigsaw to make the cuts. Be sure to raise the piece up off the bench or you'll foul the jigsaw blade.

3 Make a pattern for one half of the decorative piece of trim and then use it to mark out the detail. This will ensure that both sides are identical.

With your T-square jig and circular saw, mill the dadoes and rabbets for the shelves on the single board that will become the two sides. With a sharp chisel, clean out any remaining waste. Then rip the board in two to form the two sides.

Although I used half-dowels glued to the shelves to act as plate rails, as an option you could build square rails running across the front of each shelf area. To do this, stand the sides on edge, front edge up, clamp them together, and lay out the positions for the two rail dadoes. Then use your T-square jig and circular saw to mill the two dadoes.

If you opt to build the unit as shown in the technical drawing, then all you need to do is trim the two plate strips to length and with a little glue and a couple of ¾" brads, fasten them in place on the shelves roughly 3" away from the back edge.

Set one of the sides on the bench, dado side up, and using a little glue, set the shelves in place in the dadoes. You can further strengthen the joints by toenailing a couple of 1¼" drywall screws into it from the underside of the shelves. Then apply a little glue to the dadoes in the other side and set it in place. Clamp the structure and lay it flat on the bench, front up, and measure the diagonals to ensure the structure is square and true. If not, make adjustments by angling one of the clamps so that you can squeeze the long dimension (see photo 4).

If you opted for the square plate rails, now's the time to apply a little glue to the inside of the rail dadoes, set the rails in place, clamp them and wait until the glue has fully cured (see photo 5).

4 After you've built the shelves into the sides, measure the diagonals to ensure the basic rack is square and true. If not, make any necessary adjustments.

5 As an option, you could use square front-mounted plate rails rather than the half-dowels I used. If you decide to go this route, cut out the dadoes for the square rails and glue the rails in place in their notches. Apply clamps and leave the structure until the glue has fully cured.

Sand the single piece of stock that will form the crown, taking care to ease all the sharp edges (see photo 6). Then with six 1¼" drywall screws, attach the crown to the top from the inside, making sure the back edge is flush with the top edge, and the two ends are equidistant from the sides (see photos 7 & 8).

Do any necessary finishing sanding, making sure to remove all of the sharp edges, and then decide how you're going to finish the piece. You can either apply a stain, as I did, and a couple of coats of clear gloss polyurethane for protection, or you can paint it. Finally, fasten the two hangers in place at the back edge of the crown and top shelf.

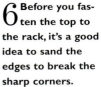

6 Before you fasten the top to the rack, it's a good idea to sand the edges to break the sharp corners.

7 Fasten the top in place using a little glue and several 1¼" drywall screws from the inside.

8 Glue the trim in place and apply clamps until the glue has fully cured.

ADHESIVE	ADVANTAGES	DISADVANTAGES	COMMON USES	WORKING TIME	CLAMPING TIME *(at 70° F)*	CURE TIME	SOLVENT
Yellow glue (aliphatic resin)	Easy to use; water resistant; water cleanup; economical.	Not waterproof (don't use on outdoor furniture).	All-purpose wood glue for interior use; stronger bond than white glue.	5 to 7 minutes	1 to 2 hours	24 hours	Warm water
Contact cement	Bonds parts immediately.	Can't readjust parts after contact.	Bonding wood veneer or plastic laminate to substrate.	Up to 1 hour	No clamps; parts bond on contact	–	Acetone
Super glue (Cyanoacrylate)	Bonds parts quickly.	Limited to small parts.	Bonding small parts made from a variety of materials.	30 seconds	10 to 60 seconds; clamps usually not required	30 minutes to several hours	Acetone
Epoxy glue	Good gap filler; waterproof; fast setting formulas available; can be used to bond glass to metal or wood.	Requires mixing.	Bonding small parts made from a variety of materials.	5 to 60 minutes depending on epoxy formula	5 minutes to several hours depending on epoxy formula	3 hours and longer	Lacquer thinner
Animal glue, dry (hide glue)	Extended working time; water cleanup; economical.	Must be mixed with water and heated; poor moisture resistance (don't use on outdoor furniture).	Time-consuming assembly work; stronger bond than liquid animal glue; interior use only.	30 minutes	2 to 3 hours	24 hours	Warm water
Animal glue, liquid (hide glue)	Easy to use; extended working time; water cleanup; economical.	Poor moisture resistance (don't use on outdoor furniture).	Time-consuming assembly work; interior use only.	5 minutes	2 hours	24 hours	Warm water
Polyurethane	Fully waterproof; gap-filling.	Eye and skin irritant.	Multi-purpose, interior and exterior applications including wood to wood, ceramic, plastic, Corian, stone, metal.	30 minutes	1 to 2 hours	8 hours	Mineral spirits while wet; must abrade or scrape off when dry.
White glue (polyvinyl acetate)	Easy to use; economical.	Not waterproof (don't use on outdoor furniture).	All-purpose wood glue for interior use; yellow glue has stronger bond.	3 to 5 minutes	16 hours	24 to 48 hours	Warm water and soap
Waterproof glue (resorcinol)	Fully waterproof; extended working time.	Requires mixing; dark color shows glue line on most woods; long clamping time.	Outdoor furniture, marine applications.	20 minutes	1 hour	12 hours	Cool water before hardening
Plastic resin (urea formaldehyde)	Good water resistance; economical.	Requires mixing; long clamping time.	Outdoor furniture, cutting boards.	15 to 30 minutes	6 hours	24 hours	Warm water and soap before hardening

16

Message
Center

Every kitchen needs one of these handy little units. This one is especially useful because it incorporates a couple of drawers where you can store small necessaries, such as matches, candles or fuses; there's even hooks where you can hang your car keys, a letter rack and two clothes pins where you can clip messages. It's made entirely from framing lumber, but you will need to rip the narrow pieces from one of the larger sizes. This project is quite easy, and can be completed over a weekend with only basic woodworking skills.

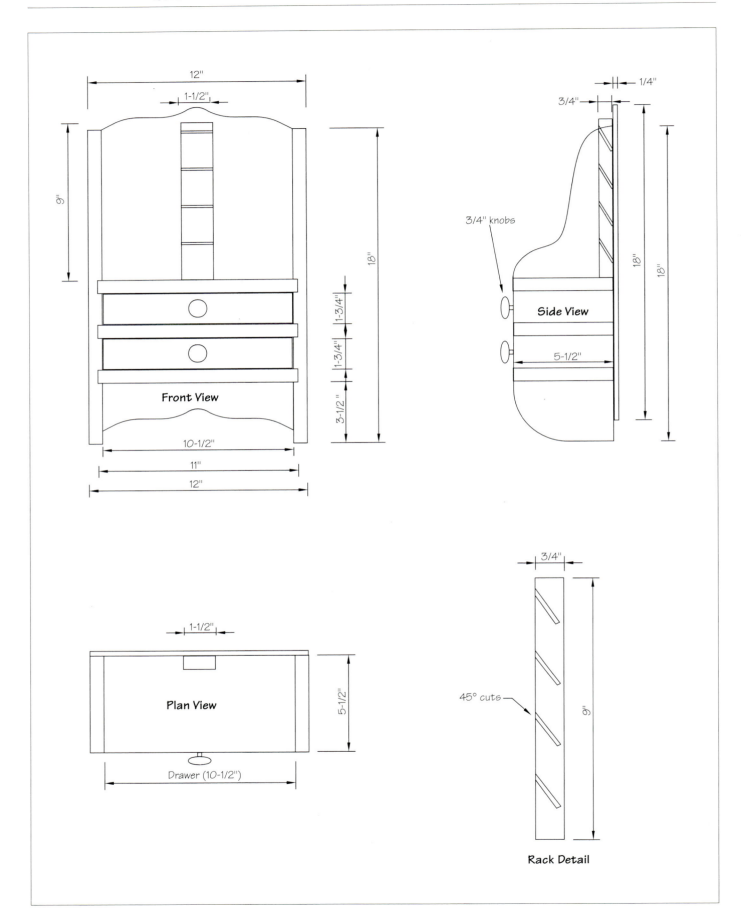

Front View

Side View

3/4" knobs

Plan View

Drawer (10-1/2")

Rack Detail

45° cuts

Cutting List • Message Center

REF.	QTY.	PART	STOCK	THICK	WIDTH	LENGTH	COMMENTS
	1	Back	Plywood	$3/8$	12	18	
	2	Sides	1x6	$3/4$	$5^1/2$	18	
	3	Shelves	1x6	$3/4$	$5^1/2$	11	
	2	Drawer Fronts	1x6	$3/4$	$1^3/4$	$10^1/2$	
	4	Drawer Sides	1x6	$3/4$	$1^3/4$	$5^1/4$	
	2	Drawer Backs	1x6	$3/4$	$1^3/8$	$8^1/2$	
	2	Drawer Bottoms	Plywood	$1/4$	9	6	
	1	Rack	1x2	$3/4$	$1^1/2$	9	

Hardware

		Brad Nails				1	
		Drywall Screws				$5/8$	
		Drywall Screws				$1^1/4$	

REQUIRED TOOLS

Table or circular saw

T-Square Jig

Drill

Screwdriver

Jigsaw or bandsaw

Measuring Tape

Straight edge

Clamps

Construction Steps

Cut all the pieces to length as per the materials list. When cutting the sides, place the two pieces together and mark out the curved detail at the bottom.

Use a straight edge and your circular saw to rip the narrow sections, including the drawer parts, from the 1×6 stock. Then lay the two sides, inside up on the bench, and mark the positions of dadoes and rabbets. Clamp the two sides together, and with your T-square jig and circular saw, mill the dadoes and rabbets. Clean away any waste with a sharp chisel.

Make a pattern from a small piece of ¼" plywood and mark out the details at the bottom of the sides (see photo 1). With your jigsaw, cut out the details and sand the sides smooth (see photo 2 & 3).

Set one of the sides on the bench, dado side up, and using a little glue, set the shelves in place in the dadoes (see photo 4). Apply a little glue to the dadoes in the other side and set it in place on the other end of the shelves. Clamp the structure and lay it flat on the bench, front up (see photo 5). Measure the diagonals to ensure the structure is square and true. Let everything cure.Cut out the details for the plywood back and set it in place (see photos 6 & 7). Use 1" brad nails to fasten it securely.

1 Use a plywood pattern to mark out the detail to the top of the two sides.

2 Fasten the two sections together with a couple of nails through the waste area. This will ensure that, when you make the cuts, the two sides will be identical. Make the cut at the bottom first, then cut where the screws are.

3 When the final cut has been made, the two side sections will separate leaving two identical sides.

4 Apply glue to the dadoes in preparation for assembling the shelves to the sides.

5 Set the shelves in place in the dadoes, then apply clamps until the glue has fully cured.

6 Use a pattern to mark out the detail on the plywood back.

7 After you've made the cuts, itís a good idea to sand the back smooth before you assemble it to the body of the center.

8 Fasten the letter rack to the back of the center with a couple of ⅝" drywall screws.

9 When you've completed cutting and milling the drawer sections, this is what you should have.

10 Use a single 1¼" drywall screw to fasten the side in place in the rabbet in the drawer front.

11 When you've fasten both side sections in place, set the back of the drawer in position and secure it with a drywall screw.

Set the angle of cut on your circular saw to 45° and cut the slots in the letter rack. Apply a little carpenterís glue to the back of the letter rack, then set it in place in the center of the back panel. Clamp it and set it aside until the glue has fully cured (see photo 8).

Now we'll build the drawers. First, take the two pieces that will form the drawer fronts and, using your circular saw and tee square jig, cut the rabbets at each end (see photo 9). Use a straight edge and your circular saw to cut the slot along the bottoms of the two fronts and four sides that will receive the plywood bottoms. The slot should be ¼" deep and ¼" wide, which means you'll need to make two cuts down the grain side-by-side. Not a difficult task, if you take your time.

Fasten the sides to the fronts, and with a little glue in the rabbets, fasten the drawer sides to the false fronts using a couple of small finishing nails at each joint (see photo 10). Then set the drawer backs in positions (see photo 11). Clamp the drawers and set them aside until the glue has fully cured.

Once the glue has dried, take the drawers out of the clamps and try them in their slots to make sure they slide in and out freely. Then slide in the plywood drawer bottoms and fasten them with a couple of small nails along the back of the drawers—there's no need to nail the sides (see photo 12). All that's left now is to fasten the knobs to the drawers, do a little final sanding, and then apply some finish. When sanding, start with 80-grit sandpaper and finish with 150-grit. Make sure you remove all the tool marks.

12 Fasten the bottom of the drawer in place in its slot with a couple of small brads.

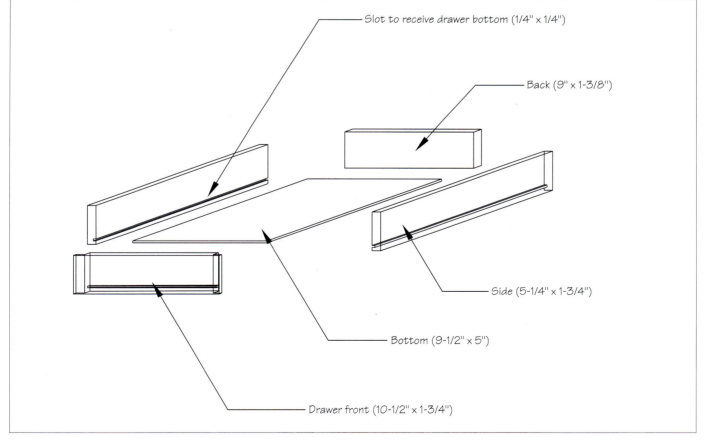

Slot to receive drawer bottom (1/4" x 1/4")

Back (9" x 1-3/8")

Side (5-1/4" x 1-3/4")

Bottom (9-1/2" x 5")

Drawer front (10-1/2" x 1-3/4")

17

Finishing
Ideas

Though finishes have been suggested for every project in this book, there are many options available to make each piece as unique as you want. From country colors to bright, modern finishes, you are unlimited in how you want your piece to look. Murals, decorative effects, stripes or decals all lend themselves to simple, fun designs that can spice up any project, either one in this book or something you have yet to design. Let your imagination run free, and create to your heart's content!

Decorating the Blanket Chest

Decorative painting is a rich and varied art form, with roots deep in many painting traditions, such as tole painting, folk art, traditional craftsmen's decoration and more. Decorative painting transforms any piece, be it a small piece of furniture, a hat box, or quilt rack, into something that is much more than its utilitarian form.

With decorative painting, the only limits you are faced with are what your particular tastes are. Take for example the blanket chest described in chapter 5, and shown to the left. This piece was painted by decorative artist Heather Dakota. She has a love of nature and the simple pleasures of life, so her painting style reflects her personal likes and tastes.

The following photographs follow Heather along as she paints the blanket chest. Remember that the subject matter is purely subjective—paint what appeals to you personally. Take these steps and use them to guide you through decorating any of the pieces in this book.

1 First, paint the entire chest deep red and let dry. Then, take a 1-inch foam brush and paint the squares that run along the bottom of the chest.

2 Next, using 2-inch low tack tape place the tape spaced every two-inches for the first layer of Buffalo Plaid on the top of the chest. Using a 2-inch foam brush and black paint, paint in between the tape. When this layer has dried, remove the tape.

3 Do the same thing in the opposite direction to make the top look like a Buffalo Plaid blanket. Again, when the paint is dry remove the tape to reveal the striping. This works for lattice work and checkerboards as well.

4 Make an oval on the front of the chest and begin to paint your scene. Choose any scene that appeals to you. Paint the background elements first and remember they don't need a lot of detail at this point.

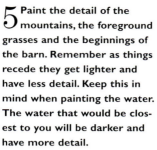

5 Paint the detail of the mountains, the foreground grasses and the beginnings of the barn. Remember as things recede they get lighter and have less detail. Keep this in mind when painting the water. The water that would be closest to you will be darker and have more detail.

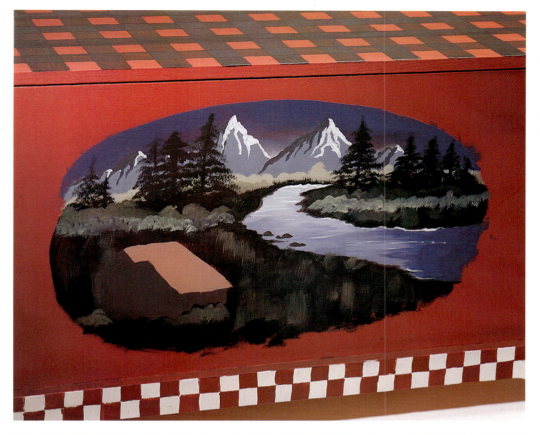

6 Lastly, add in the foreground details by finishing the cabin with shadows and highlights. Paint the trees using a scruffy brush and add the details with progressively lighter greens. Add in the tree limb from the left, the fence post on the right and the rocks in the water. Don't forget the shading and highlighting for the pieces to look real. When you're done, add a twig border around your scene using a no. 2 script liner and brown paint.

index

More of the best project books for woodworkers!

Build Your Own Kitchen Cabinets
Superbly detailed, this one-of-kind book makes kitchen cabinet-making accessible to you, no matter what your level of skill. Packed with step-by-step instructions and the guidance you need for the project you want. #70376/$22.99/136 pages/170+ b&w illus, 8p 4-color insert/paperback

Build Your Own Entertainment Centers
With three basic designs and four different styles, you can customize the construction and design of entertainment centers that fit your skill level, tools, style and budget. An exceptional project book. #70354/$22.99/128 pages/229 B&W illus/paperback

The Woodworker's Guide to Furniture Design
This practical reference makes creating beautiful, well-proportioned furniture easy by teaching the fundamentals of good design, with step-by-step instruction for developing furniture ideas into fully functional plans. #70355/$27.99/208 pages/110 b&w illus

Making Wooden Mechanical Models
Discover plans for 15 handsome and incredibly clever machines with visible wheels, cranks, pistons and other moving parts make of wood. Expertly photographed and complete with materials lists and diagrams, the plans call for a challenging variety of techniques and procedures. #70288/$21.99/144 pages/341 illus./paperback

Making More Wooden Mechanical Models
Turn the cranks, press the buttons and pull the levers on 15 projects that make great gifts. Despite their seemingly elaborate configurations, they're simple to make following this guide's complete step-by-step instructions. You'll find that every project features a full-color close up of the finished piece, in addition to hand-rendered drawings, cutting lists and special tips for making difficult steps easier. #70444/$24.99/128 pages/15 color, 250 b&w illus/paperback

Beautiful Wooden Gifts You Can Make in a Weekend
This fun and unique book offers you 20 different gift projects that can be built in a couple of days, including step-by-step instructions for jewelry boxes, toys, kitchen accessories, puzzle boxes and more. An easy-to-follow format includes line drawings, photos, illustrations and complete tools and materials lists. #70384/$22.99/128 pages/20 color, 160 b&w illus./paperback

The Woodworker's Visual Guide to Pricing Your Work
With this illustrated pricing guide, you'll be sure to get the best prices for your projects, no matter what your specialty. Each price is determined using proven formulas that factor in labor, materials, overhead and current market value. In addition, you'll receive prac-

tical advice about selling and marketing, such as how to run a successful craft show, how to get into juried exhibitions, and how to close a sale. #70443/$21.99/128 pages/200 b&w photos/paperback

Smart Shelving & Storage Solutions
These innovative and inexpensive storage solutions are perfect for do-it-yourselfers. From book shelves, chests and cabinets to armoires, closet systems and benches, you'll find more than 27 woodworking projects to help you make the most of your space—whether it's under the bed, over the sink or in the garage. #70445/$24.99/144 pages/360 color, 40 b&w illus./paperback

The Weekend Woodworker
A fantastic resource for the straightforward, step-by-step projects you like! This book offers you a range of attractive challenges, from smaller items—such as a stylish CD rack, mailbox or birdhouse—to larger, easy-to-assemble projects including a wall cupboard, child's bed, computer workstation or coffee table. Each project provides clear and easy step-by-step instructions, photographs and diagrams, ideal for both the beginner and expert. #70456/$22.99/144 pages/200 color photos/paperback

How to Build Classic Garden Furniture
This easy, step-by-step guide will have you anxious to begin crafting this elegant outdoor furniture. The 20 projects are designed to withstand years of outdoor exposure with minimal care, and are versatile enough to compliment any home's style. Each beautiful piece is made easy to accomplish with full-color illustrations, numbered steps, close-up photos and alternatives for design, wood selection and finishing. #70395/$24.99/128 pages/275 color, 69 b&w illus./paperback

How to Design and Build Your Ideal Woodshop
Designed especially for the home-shop woodworker, this guide features dozens of practical alternatives, tips and solutions for transforming attics, garages, basements or out-buildings into efficient and safe woodshops. Clear instructions also include photos, drawings and considerations for electricity,

lighting, ventilation, plumbing, accessibility, insulation, flooring and more. #70397/$24.99/160 pages/paperback

Building Classic Antique Furniture with Pine
This book offers a range of affordable and user-friendly furniture projects, including antique-style tables, desks, cabinets, boxes, chests and more. Each step-by-step project includes numbered steps with photos and drawings, material lists, a brief description of the function and history of each piece as well as the estimated current market value of both the original piece and the reproduction. #70396/$22.99/144 pages/216 color illus./paperback

The Woodworker's Guide to Shop Math
A perfect companion to The Woodworking Handbook, this hands-on guide rakes mathematic principles from the chalkboard to the wood shop, using real-life shop situations to make math easy and practical. Also provided is an overview of basic arithmetic, a review of common units of measurement, and several conversion charts and tables for fractions, multiplication, weighrs, decimals, volume, area, temperature and more. #70406/$22.99/208 pages/169 b&w illus./paperback

Making Elegant Gifts from Wood
Develop your woodworking skills and make over 30 gift-quality projects at the same time? You'll find everything you're looking to create in your gifts—variety, timeless styles, pleasing proportions and imaginative designs that call for the best woods. Plus, technique sidebars and hardware installation tips make your job even easier. #70331/$24.99/128 pages/30 color, 120 b&w illus.

Good Wood Handbook, Second Edition
Now in paperback! This handy reference gives you all the information you need to select and use the right wood for the job - before you buy. You'll discover valuable information on a wide selection of commercial softwoods and hardwoods—from common uses, color and grain to how the wood glues and takes finish. #70451/$14.99/128 pages/250 color illus./paperback